DONISE BOYD

The Art of Intentional Communication

Word's That Build, Not Break

This book was professionally typeset on Reedsy.
Find out more at reedsy.com

To my family—
the ones who laid the foundation beneath every word I speak.

You taught me that communication is more than language;
it is presence, patience, and the courage to listen with an open heart.

Your examples of grace, resilience, and truth-telling shaped the way I show up in
the world.
Every chapter of this book carries your fingerprints,
your wisdom,
your love.

Thank you for giving me the roots to speak with intention
and the wings to teach others to do the same.

Contents

Preface

❧ A Note to the Reader

Before you turn the page, I want to honor the courage it takes to pick up a book about communication.

Most of us were never taught how to speak from a grounded place, how to listen beneath the surface, or how to repair the moments when our words miss the mark. We learned by watching, absorbing, surviving, and doing the best we could with what we had. If you're here, it means you're ready to do more than communicate — you're ready to **connect**.

This book is not about perfection. It's about presence. It's about intention. It's about choosing words that build, even when emotions run high. It's about learning to speak from your truth instead of your triggers, and to hold space for others without losing yourself.

As you move through these pages, I invite you to slow down. Reflect. Breathe. Notice what rises in you — the resistance, the relief, the recognition. Every reaction is information. Every insight is an opening.

My hope is that this book becomes a companion you return to in the moments that matter most — the hard conversations, the tender ones, the ones that shape your relationships and your legacy.

Thank you for trusting me to walk with you. Thank you for choosing to grow. And thank you for believing that your words can be a place of safety, truth, and connection.

You're exactly where you need to be.

Acknowledgments

A note of gratitude

To the people who raised me — my mother, my father, my grandparents, and my aunts and uncles: Your patience, your grace, and your quiet strength shaped the soil I grew from. Your words, your wisdom, and your presence live in every chapter of this book. This work is an extension of your legacy.

To my family: Thank you for your love, your laughter, and your willingness to grow with me. You are my grounding place and my greatest classroom.

To every mother, father, partner, friend, leader, and human who has ever questioned their voice: This book is for you. May you find clarity, compassion, and courage in these pages. May your words build, not break. May your communication become part of your healing — and your legacy.

And to every reader who trusted me with your heart: Thank you. Your intention matters. Your voice matters. Your growth matters. I am honored to walk this journey with you.

Introduction

Why Your Words Matter More Than You Think

We live in a world overflowing with words. They fill our homes, our group chats, our meetings, our memories. We speak them, type them, whisper them, and sometimes hold them back until they become heavy inside us. And yet, for all the words we use, so many of us still struggle to feel understood — or to express ourselves in ways that honor both our truth and our relationships.

Communication is something we do every day, but intentional communication is something we must learn.

Most of us were not taught how to speak from a grounded place. We weren't shown how to slow down long enough to understand what we're really feeling before we respond. We weren't given language for our needs, our boundaries, or our emotional patterns. Instead, we learned communication the way we learned everything else in childhood: by watching the people who raised us, absorbing their rhythms, their silences, their reactions, and their ways of navigating conflict or connection.

Some of what we learned helped us. Some of it protected us. Some of it shaped us in ways we are only now beginning to understand.

This book is an invitation to pause and look beneath the surface of your words — not with judgment, but with curiosity. Because every conversation carries more than what is spoken. It carries intention. It carries history. It carries the emotional habits we've built over years of surviving, loving, and trying our best.

Intentional communication is not about being perfect. It's about being present.

It's about choosing words that build instead of break, even when emotions run high. It's about learning to speak from your truth instead of your triggers. It's about understanding the intention behind your voice — and recognizing the intention behind someone else's.

When we communicate without intention, we react. When we communicate with intention, we connect.

This book will guide you through that shift.

You'll explore the seven intention styles — the patterns that shape how you show up in conversations, especially when you feel stressed, misunderstood, or emotionally charged. You'll learn how to recognize your default style, how to soften the habits that no longer serve you, and how to cultivate the intention style that builds trust, clarity, and emotional safety.

You'll practice speaking in ways that honor what you feel *and* what you value. You'll learn how to listen for what's not being said. You'll discover how to repair conversations that went wrong, and how to create new patterns that strengthen your relationships instead of straining them.

Most importantly, you'll learn how to use your words as tools for connection — with yourself, with the people you love, and with the communities you're part of.

Your words carry power. Your presence carries weight. Your intention shapes your legacy.

And you don't have to navigate any of it alone. I'm honored to walk with you through these pages, and I'm grateful you've chosen to begin this journey.

Let's step into the art of intentional communication — together.

I

Part I — The Foundation of Intentional Communication

Before we can change the way we communicate, we must understand the forces that shaped us.
Every one of us learned to speak, listen, react, and respond long before we had the language to describe what we were doing. We absorbed communication the way children absorb everything — through observation, imitation, and survival. We learned from the tone of the household, the rhythm of conversations, the pauses between sentences, and the emotional climate we grew up in.

1

What We Really Mean When We Speak

Understanding the layers beneath every conversation

We often think communication begins with words — the sentences we form, the tone we choose, the timing we hope is right. But the truth is, communication begins long before sound ever leaves our mouths. It begins in the quiet places inside us: our beliefs, our fears, our memories, our expectations, and the emotional patterns we've carried for years.

Most of us speak from layers we've never named.

We speak from the way we were raised.

We speak from what we needed but didn't receive.

We speak from the moments that shaped us — the tender ones and the painful ones.

We speak from habits we didn't choose but learned to survive.

And because we rarely slow down to examine those layers, we often misunderstand ourselves just as much as we misunderstand others.

This chapter is an invitation to pause and look beneath the surface of your words — not to judge yourself, but to understand yourself. Because when you understand what's happening inside you, you gain the power to communicate with intention instead of instinct.

๑ The Unseen Conversation Happening Inside You

Every external conversation is shaped by an internal one.

Before you respond to your partner, your child, your coworker, or your friend, something happens within you. A thought. A feeling. A memory. A fear. A hope. A need. A story you've told yourself about what this moment means.

You may not notice it, but it's there.

- When someone interrupts you, you may feel dismissed — not because of the interruption itself, but because of a lifetime of feeling unheard.
- When someone questions you, you may feel attacked — not because of their tone, but because you've spent years proving your worth.
- When someone expresses disappointment, you may feel responsible — not because you did something wrong, but because you've been conditioned to keep the peace.

Our reactions are rarely about the moment in front of us.

They are about the meaning we attach to it.

Intentional communication begins with recognizing that meaning.

๑ The Stories We Carry Into Every Conversation

We all carry stories — internal narratives that shape how we interpret what others say.

Some of these stories sound like:

- *"I have to defend myself."*
- *"I don't want to upset anyone."*
- *"I need to prove I'm capable."*
- *"I can't let them see me struggle."*

- *"If I don't stay in control, everything will fall apart."*

These stories are not weaknesses. They are survival strategies — formed in childhood, reinforced in adulthood, and often invisible to us.

But when we become aware of them, we gain the power to choose a new story.

๛ Why Awareness Matters More Than Perfection

You don't need to communicate perfectly to communicate intentionally.

You simply need to be aware.

Awareness gives you options.

Awareness gives you pause.

Awareness gives you the ability to respond instead of react.

When you understand what's happening inside you, you can:

- name your feelings instead of acting them out
- express your needs instead of hinting at them
- set boundaries without guilt
- listen without defensiveness
- speak without fear
- repair without shame

Awareness is the foundation of every skill you will learn in this book.

๛ The First Step: Seeing Yourself Clearly

Before we explore the intention styles, before we practice new communication tools, before we step into the real-life application of these skills, we begin here — with self-awareness.

This chapter is your mirror.

Not a harsh one.

Not a critical one.
A compassionate one.
A mirror that helps you see:

- why you speak the way you do
- what you're really trying to protect
- what you're hoping others will understand
- what you need but rarely name
- what you fear but rarely admit
- what you long for in your relationships

When you see yourself clearly, you can communicate clearly.

๛ A Gentle Reflection

Take a moment and ask yourself:

- *What do I hope people understand about me when I speak?*
- *What am I afraid people might misunderstand?*
- *What emotions rise in me most often during conversations?*
- *What do I need from others that I rarely say out loud?*

These questions are not meant to overwhelm you.

They are meant to open you.

Because the more you understand your inner world, the more intentional your outer communication becomes.

๛ Closing Thought

Communication is not just about words.

It is about awareness.

It is about intention.

It is about understanding the emotional landscape within you so you can navigate the emotional landscape between you and others.

This chapter is the beginning of that journey.

You are not here to fix yourself.

You are here to understand yourself.

And understanding is the first step toward transformation.

🌿 Reflection Prompts

✧ Self-Reflection

- What emotions rise in me most often during conversations, and where do I feel them in my body?
- What do I hope people understand about me when I speak?
- What am I afraid people might misunderstand?
- What patterns do I notice in my reactions when I feel unheard, dismissed, or misunderstood?
- What stories from my past might be shaping how I communicate today?

✧ *Connection Reflection*

- When was the last time I felt truly understood? What made that moment feel safe?
- When was the last time I misunderstood someone else? What assumptions did I make?
- How do I want people to feel after talking with me?

CHAPTER 1 SUMMARY— WHAT WE REALLY MEAN WHEN WE SPEAK

- Communication begins long before words.
- Our reactions are rooted in past experiences, unspoken needs, and emotional patterns.

- Awareness is the foundation of intentional communication.
- When we understand ourselves, we can communicate with clarity and compassion.
- The first step: see yourself with honesty and gentleness.

2

The Hidden Agenda: How Unspoken Needs Shape Our Words

Understanding what you're really asking for when you speak

Every conversation carries a need — even when we don't say it out loud.

Sometimes the need is simple: to be heard, to be understood, to be respected.

Other times, the need is more tender: to feel safe, to feel valued, to feel chosen, to feel like we matter.

But because most of us were never taught to name our needs, we learned to communicate around them instead of through them. We hint. We hope. We assume. We react. We protect. We perform. We please. We prove. We plan. We do everything except say the thing we actually need.

This chapter is an invitation to bring those hidden needs into the light — not to expose your vulnerability, but to honor it.

Because your needs are not weaknesses. They are signals. They are information. They are the quiet truths guiding your communication.

᧣ Every Reaction Has a Root

When someone's tone feels sharp, when a question feels like criticism, when silence feels like rejection — your reaction is rarely about the moment itself. It's about the need underneath the moment.

For example:

- If you feel dismissed easily, your hidden need may be *to feel heard.*
- If you get defensive quickly, your hidden need may be *to feel respected.*
- If you shut down during conflict, your hidden need may be *to feel safe.*
- If you over-explain, your hidden need may be *to feel understood.*
- If you avoid asking for help, your hidden need may be *to feel capable.*

Your reactions are not random. They are rooted in unmet needs.

When you understand the root, you can change the reaction.

᧣ The Cost of Unspoken Needs

Unspoken needs don't disappear. They leak out.

They show up in:

- tone
- sarcasm
- withdrawal
- overexplaining
- defensiveness
- people-pleasing
- shutting down
- trying to control the moment
- trying to avoid the moment

When needs go unspoken, communication becomes a guessing game — and guessing games lead to misunderstanding, resentment, and emotional distance.

But when needs are named, communication becomes clear, honest, and grounded.

๛ Why We Struggle to Name Our Needs

Most of us were taught to hide our needs long before we had the language to express them.

Maybe you learned:

- that asking for what you need was "too much"
- that expressing emotion made others uncomfortable
- that being strong meant being silent
- that keeping the peace mattered more than being honest
- that your needs didn't matter unless they benefited someone else

So you adapted. You learned to communicate in ways that protected you — even if they didn't connect you.

This chapter is not about blaming your past. It's about understanding how it shaped your voice.

๛ Naming Your Needs Without Shame

Naming your needs is not selfish. It is responsible.

It gives others a chance to show up for you. It gives you a chance to show up for yourself.

Here are a few needs that often hide beneath our words:

- *I need reassurance.*
- *I need clarity.*
- *I need time to process.*
- *I need to feel safe before I can open up.*
- *I need to know you're listening.*

- *I need to feel respected.*
- *I need to feel like we're on the same team.*

When you name your need, you remove the guesswork. You remove the tension. You remove the emotional fog.

You make connection possible.

᧞ A Gentle Practice: Before You Speak, Ask Yourself...

Before responding in a conversation, pause and ask:

- *What do I need right now?*
- *What am I hoping they understand?*
- *What am I afraid they might misunderstand?*
- *What emotion is rising in me?*
- *What am I trying to protect?*

These questions help you shift from reaction to intention.

They help you speak from your truth instead of your fear.

᧞ Closing Thought

Your needs are not burdens. They are bridges.

When you learn to name them, you create space for deeper connection, clearer communication, and more honest relationships.

This chapter is your permission to stop hiding what you need and start honoring it.

Because when your needs are seen, your voice becomes free.

❧ Reflection Prompts

✧ Self-Reflection

- What need was I trying to express the last time I felt triggered in a conversation?
- Which needs do I struggle to name out loud? Why?
- What emotions do I tend to hide, and what do I fear might happen if I expressed them?
- What patterns do I notice when my needs go unmet?

✧ Connection Reflection

- How do I respond when someone else expresses a need?
- What would it feel like to communicate my needs without apology?
- What support do I wish others would offer me more often?

CHAPTER 2 SUMMARY— THE HIDDEN AGENDA

- Every conversation carries an unspoken need.
- Unmet needs shape tone, reactions, and emotional intensity.
- Unspoken needs leak out through defensiveness, withdrawal, or overexplaining.
- Naming your needs brings clarity, connection, and emotional safety.
- Your needs are not burdens — they are bridges.

3

The Power of Intention

How your inner posture shapes every conversation

Before a single word leaves your mouth, something else speaks first: your intention.

Intention is the quiet energy behind your communication — the posture of your heart, the direction of your focus, the emotional stance you take before you open your mouth. Most people never think about their intention. They think about their point, their frustration, their fear, their need to be understood. But intention is what determines how your words land, how others feel in your presence, and whether a conversation becomes a bridge or a barrier.

This chapter is an invitation to slow down and notice the intention beneath your words — because intention is the difference between reacting and relating.

❧ Intention Is the Emotional Tone You Set Before You Speak

Every conversation begins with an internal choice, whether conscious or not:

- *Am I here to connect or to control?*

- *Am I here to understand or to defend?*
- *Am I here to listen or to win?*
- *Am I here to express or to protect?*
- *Am I here to build or to brace myself?*

Your intention shapes your tone, your body language, your facial expression, your pace, and your emotional presence. Even if your words are calm, your intention can still communicate fear, frustration, or self-protection.

People don't just hear your words. They feel your intention.

℘ When Intention Is Unclear, Communication Becomes Confusing

Have you ever said something simple, but the other person reacted strongly? Or tried to express a concern, but it came out sounding like criticism? Or attempted to set a boundary, but it felt like a fight?

That's intention at work.

When your intention is unclear — even to you — your communication becomes mixed:

- You want connection, but your tone sounds defensive.
- You want clarity, but your questions sound like accusations.
- You want reassurance, but your silence feels like withdrawal.
- You want honesty, but your delivery feels harsh.

The problem isn't your desire. It's the unspoken intention behind it.

℘ Intention Is Not the Same as Outcome

You can have a loving intention and still create tension. You can have a fearful intention and still sound calm. You can have a protective intention and still push someone away.

Intention is not about perfection. It's about awareness.

When you know your intention, you can adjust it. When you don't, your patterns take over.

☙ The Most Common Intentions We Bring Into Conversations

Here are a few intentions that often guide communication without us realizing it:

- **To protect yourself**
- **To avoid conflict**
- **To be right**
- **To be understood**
- **To keep the peace**
- **To control the outcome**
- **To not disappoint anyone**
- **To feel safe**
- **To feel valued**
- **To feel respected**

None of these intentions are wrong. They are human.

But when they go unexamined, they can lead to miscommunication, emotional distance, and unnecessary conflict.

☙ Shifting Your Intention Changes Everything

When you pause long enough to ask, *"What is my intention right now?"* you create space for choice.

You can shift from:

- **defending** to **understanding**
- **reacting** to **responding**
- **controlling** to **connecting**
- **pleasing** to **expressing**

- **avoiding** to **engaging**
- **proving** to **sharing**

This shift doesn't require a long process. It requires a moment of awareness. A breath. A pause. A softening. A choosing.

᠊ A Simple Practice: Set Your Intention Before You Speak

Before entering a conversation — especially one that feels tender, important, or emotionally charged — ask yourself:

- *What do I want to create in this moment?*
- *What do I want the other person to feel?*
- *What do I want to feel?*
- *What matters most here — connection or control?*
- *What is the outcome I'm hoping for?*

These questions help you anchor your intention so your words can follow your heart instead of your habits.

᠊ The Intention That Changes Everything: Partnership

The most transformative intention in communication is partnership — the desire to understand, connect, and work together rather than win, avoid, or protect.

Partnership says:

- *We're on the same team.*
- *We can figure this out together.*
- *Your feelings matter and so do mine.*
- *I'm here to understand, not attack.*
- *I want connection more than control.*

This intention softens your tone, opens your body language, and creates emotional safety — even in hard conversations.

Partnership is the intention that turns communication into connection.

๛ Closing Thought

Intention is the quiet force shaping every conversation you have. When you learn to set your intention with awareness, your communication becomes clearer, kinder, and more grounded.

You don't need perfect words. You need a clear heart.

Because when your intention is aligned with connection, your words naturally follow.

๛ Reflection Prompts

✧ *Self-Reflection*

- What intention do I most often bring into conversations: connection, control, protection, or avoidance?
- How does my intention shift when I feel stressed or overwhelmed?
- What intention do I want to lead with more often?
- What happens in my body when my intention is unclear?

✧ *Connection Reflection*

- How do others respond when my intention is defensive or protective?
- What conversations feel easier when I set my intention first?
- What intention would create more emotional safety in my relationships?

CHAPTER 3 SUMMARY — THE POWER OF INTENTION

- Intention is the emotional tone you set before you speak
- People feel your intention even more than your words.
- Unclear intentions lead to mixed messages and misunderstandings.
- Awareness allows you to shift from reacting to relating.
- Partnership is the intention that transforms communication.

4

Words That Build, Not Break

How emotionally safe communication strengthens every relationship

Words are powerful. They can soften a moment or shatter it. They can open someone's heart or close it. They can build trust or break connection.

Most of us don't realize how much weight our words carry — not because we're careless, but because we're human. We speak from our emotions, our habits, our fears, and our unspoken needs. And without intention, even well-meaning words can land in ways we never intended.

This chapter is an invitation to become more aware of the emotional impact of your words — not to censor yourself, but to communicate in ways that create safety, clarity, and connection.

✎ Words Carry Emotional Weight

Every word you speak carries energy. Your tone, your pace, your facial expression, your posture — they all shape how your words are received.

For example:

- "What?" can sound curious or irritated.
- "I'm fine" can sound peaceful or resentful.

- "We need to talk" can sound grounding or threatening.
- "I didn't mean it like that" can sound clarifying or dismissive.

The same words can build or break depending on the intention behind them and the emotional state of the person receiving them.

This is why emotional safety matters.

⌇ What Is Emotionally Safe Communication?

Emotionally safe communication is not about being soft or passive. It's about being clear, grounded, and considerate of how your words land.

Emotionally safe communication:

- honors your truth
- respects the other person's experience
- creates space for both people to be honest
- reduces defensiveness
- builds trust
- strengthens connection

It's not about avoiding hard conversations. It's about approaching them with care.

⌇ The Difference Between Building and Breaking

Words that **build** sound like:

- "Help me understand."
- "I hear you."
- "I want us to figure this out together."
- "This is important to me."
- "I need a moment to gather my thoughts."

Words that **break** often sound like:

- "You always…"
- "You never…"
- "What's wrong with you?"
- "Forget it."
- "Whatever."

Breaking words shut down connection. Building words open it.

And the difference is rarely about vocabulary — it's about intention, tone, and emotional presence.

๛ Why We Sometimes Use Words That Break

We don't use harmful words because we're bad people. We use them because we're overwhelmed, afraid, triggered, or trying to protect ourselves.

Breaking words often come from:

- feeling unheard
- feeling disrespected
- feeling misunderstood
- feeling out of control
- feeling emotionally flooded
- feeling unappreciated

When you understand the emotion behind your words, you can choose a different response.

๛ Building Words Require Slowing Down

You cannot build when you're rushing. You cannot build when you're triggered. You cannot build when you're trying to win.

Building words come from:

- pausing
- breathing
- grounding
- choosing intention
- remembering the relationship matters more than the moment

This is the heart of intentional communication.

✏ A Simple Practice: The Building Pause

Before responding, ask yourself:

- *Will these words build or break?*
- *What am I trying to protect right now?*
- *What do I want the other person to feel?*
- *What outcome do I actually want?*

This pause is not weakness. It is wisdom.

✏ Closing Thought

Your words are seeds. They take root in the hearts of the people you love. They shape how safe others feel with you. They shape how deeply you connect. They shape the emotional legacy you leave behind.

When you choose words that build, you create relationships that last.

🌿 Reflection Prompts

✦ Self-Reflection

- What words or tones do I use when I feel overwhelmed or unheard?
- Which of my communication habits tend to break connection?
- Which habits help build connection?

• What emotions usually sit underneath my sharpest words?

✧ *Connection Reflection*

• How do I want people to feel after talking with me?
• What building phrases could I use more often?
• What breaking phrases do I want to retire?

CHAPTER 4 SUMMARY — WORDS THAT BUILD, NOT BREAK

• Words carry emotional weight.
• Emotionally safe communication builds trust and connection.
• Breaking words come from fear, overwhelm, or unmet needs.
• Building words come from intention, clarity, and presence.
• Your words are seeds — choose the ones that grow connection.

II

❧ Part II — The Seven Intention Styles

Before we can change the way we communicate, we must understand how we communicate — especially in the moments when emotions rise, pressure builds, or old patterns take over.

Every one of us has an intention style: a familiar way of showing up in conversations when we want to be heard, understood, protected, or respected. These styles are not flaws or personality types. They are survival strategies — shaped by our upbringing, our relationships, our wounds, and our hopes.

5

The Protector

When caution becomes your communication style

The Protector shows up when life has taught you to stay alert. To anticipate disappointment. To prepare for impact. To guard your heart before anyone has the chance to hurt it.

If this is your intention style, you don't communicate to attack — you communicate to prevent. You listen for tone shifts, you read between the lines, you brace for what might go wrong. You speak with caution, clarity, and sometimes a little edge, not because you want conflict, but because you want safety.

The Protector is not a flaw. It is a response to lived experience.

This chapter is an invitation to understand the wisdom behind your vigilance — and to learn how to soften it when it no longer serves you.

᧡ Why the Protector Emerges

The Protector often develops in environments where:

- emotions were unpredictable
- trust was inconsistent

- criticism came without warning
- vulnerability was unsafe
- you had to stay "on guard" to stay okay

So you learned to:

- anticipate problems
- prepare your defense
- stay one step ahead
- read people deeply
- protect your heart at all costs

These skills helped you survive. But they can make connection feel compli-cated.

ꙮ How the Protector Communicates

When the Protector leads, communication often sounds like:

- clarifying everything
- asking pointed questions
- preparing for worst-case scenarios
- sounding firm even when you're not angry
- needing reassurance but not wanting to ask for it
- assuming others may disappoint you
- reacting quickly to perceived threats

You may notice:

- your tone gets sharper when you feel unsafe
- your body tenses when someone's words feel unclear
- you replay conversations to analyze what was "really meant"
- you struggle to trust without evidence

- you feel responsible for preventing emotional harm

The Protector is always scanning for danger — even in safe relationships.

⚘ The Hidden Need of the Protector

Beneath the vigilance is a simple, tender need:

"I need to feel safe."

Not safe as in protected from harm — safe as in emotionally held, understood, and not blindsided.

The Protector is not trying to control others. The Protector is trying to control the *unknown.*

⚘ The Strengths of the Protector

This intention style carries powerful gifts:

- You notice what others miss.
- You sense emotional shifts quickly.
- You ask thoughtful, clarifying questions.
- You protect the people you love fiercely.
- You are loyal, steady, and deeply intuitive.
- You don't run from hard truths.

When softened with awareness, the Protector becomes a grounding presence — someone others feel safe with.

⚘ The Challenges of the Protector

When the Protector is overactive, communication can feel:

- intense
- guarded

- suspicious
- defensive
- emotionally distant
- easily triggered

Others may feel like they're being interrogated when you're simply trying to understand. They may feel pushed away when you're actually trying to protect yourself.

The challenge is not your intention — it's the emotional armor.

❧ Softening the Protector Without Losing Your Strength

You don't need to silence the Protector. You need to guide it.

Here are gentle shifts that help:

- Replace assumptions with curiosity.
- Replace defensiveness with clarity.
- Replace bracing with breathing.
- Replace "What's wrong?" with "Help me understand."
- Replace "I'm fine" with "I'm feeling a little guarded right now."

These small shifts create emotional safety — for you and for others.

❧ A Grounding Practice for the Protector

Before responding, ask yourself:

- *What am I trying to protect right now?*
- *Is this moment actually unsafe, or just unfamiliar?*
- *What do I need to feel grounded?*
- *What intention do I want to lead with?*

This practice helps you respond from presence instead of protection.

๛ Closing Thought

The Protector is not here to harm you. It is here to keep you safe.

But safety and connection can coexist. You don't have to choose one or the other.

When you soften your guard — even slightly — you make room for deeper trust, clearer communication, and relationships that feel steady, honest, and emotionally secure.

❧ Reflection Prompts

✧ Self-Reflection

- When do I feel myself shifting into "Protector mode"?
- What situations make me brace or prepare for the worst?
- What am I usually trying to prevent when I get defensive?
- What does emotional safety look like for me?

✧ Connection Reflection

- How do others respond when I communicate from a guarded place?
- What helps me soften when I feel tense or suspicious?
- What would it feel like to trust without over-preparing?

CHAPTER 5 SUMMARY — THE PROTECTOR

- The Protector communicates to stay safe, not to attack.
- This style forms in environments where trust felt uncertain.
- Strengths: intuition, loyalty, clarity, emotional awareness.
- Challenges: defensiveness, intensity, guardedness.
- Softening comes from curiosity, grounding, and naming your needs.

6

The Pleaser

When harmony becomes your communication style

The Pleaser shows up when peace feels like survival. When keeping everyone comfortable feels safer than expressing your truth. When you've learned that your value is tied to how well you can anticipate, soothe, or accommodate the needs of others.

If this is your intention style, you don't communicate to manipulate — you communicate to maintain harmony. You soften your tone, shrink your needs, and adjust your words to avoid conflict or disappointment. You want connection so deeply that you sometimes sacrifice your own voice to keep it.

The Pleaser is not a weakness. It is a response to environments where your comfort depended on someone else's mood.

This chapter is an invitation to honor the tenderness behind your people-pleasing — and to reclaim your voice without losing your compassion.

ॐ Why the Pleaser Emerges

The Pleaser often develops in environments where:

- conflict felt dangerous

- emotions were unpredictable
- you were praised for being "easy" or "good"
- your needs were minimized or ignored
- you felt responsible for others' feelings
- love or approval felt conditional

So you learned to:

- read the room
- anticipate needs
- avoid tension
- smooth over discomfort
- stay agreeable
- keep everyone happy

These skills helped you stay connected. But they can make authenticity feel risky.

ૐ How the Pleaser Communicates

When the Pleaser leads, communication often sounds like:

- "It's okay, don't worry about it."
- "Whatever you want is fine."
- "I'm good, really."
- "I don't want to be a burden."
- "I just want everyone to be happy."

You may notice:

- you apologize often
- you downplay your feelings
- you avoid expressing needs

- you say yes when you want to say no
- you feel responsible for others' comfort
- you struggle to tolerate someone's disappointment
- you replay conversations to make sure you didn't upset anyone

The Pleaser communicates to maintain peace — even at the cost of your own truth.

The Hidden Need of the Pleaser

Beneath the accommodation is a tender, human need:

"I need to feel accepted and safe."

Not accepted for what you do — accepted for who you are.

The Pleaser is not trying to avoid responsibility. The Pleaser is trying to avoid rejection.

The Strengths of the Pleaser

This intention style carries beautiful gifts:

- You are empathetic and emotionally intuitive.
- You create warm, welcoming environments.
- You notice the needs of others quickly.
- You are thoughtful, considerate, and generous.
- You bring calm to tense situations.
- You value harmony and connection.

When balanced, the Pleaser becomes a compassionate communicator who brings gentleness and emotional safety to every space.

℘ The Challenges of the Pleaser

When the Pleaser is overactive, communication can feel:

- unclear
- indirect
- self-silencing
- overly accommodating
- resentful beneath the surface
- emotionally exhausting

Others may assume you're fine when you're not. They may rely on your flexibility without realizing the cost. They may never hear your true needs because you've learned to hide them.
   The challenge is not your kindness — it's the silence underneath it.

℘ Reclaiming Your Voice Without Losing Your Warmth

You don't need to stop being kind. You need to stop disappearing.
   Here are gentle shifts that help:

- Replace "It's fine" with "Here's what I actually prefer."
- Replace "Whatever you want" with "Let's find something that works for both of us."
- Replace "I don't care" with "I do have a preference."
- Replace "I'm sorry" with "Thank you for understanding."
- Replace silence with small truths spoken softly.

These shifts honor your voice without harming the connection you value.

✿ A Grounding Practice for the Pleaser

Before responding, ask yourself:

- *Am I saying this to connect or to avoid conflict?*
- *What do I actually want or need right now?*
- *What am I afraid will happen if I speak honestly?*
- *What would it feel like to trust that the relationship can handle my truth?*

This practice helps you speak from authenticity instead of fear.

✿ Closing Thought

The Pleaser is not here to erase you. It is here to protect you.

But you deserve relationships where your truth is welcome. Where your needs matter. Where your voice is not an inconvenience but a contribution.

When you speak honestly — even gently — you create connection that is real, not rehearsed.

❧ Reflection Prompts

✦ Self-Reflection

- When do I feel myself slipping into people-pleasing?
- What emotions do I avoid expressing because I fear disappointing others?
- What needs do I silence most often?
- What does my body feel like when I say yes but mean no?

✦ Connection Reflection

- How do others respond when I hide my true feelings?
- What relationships feel safe enough for me to practice honesty?
- What small truth could I express this week?

CHAPTER 6 SUMMARY — THE PLEASER

- The Pleaser communicates to maintain harmony and avoid rejection.
- This style forms in environments where conflict felt unsafe.
- Strengths: empathy, warmth, intuition, generosity.
- Challenges: self-silencing, over-accommodating, hidden resentment.
- Healing comes from expressing needs with honesty and gentleness.

7

The Performer

When being impressive becomes your communication style

The Performer shows up when you've learned that being accepted depends on being exceptional. When being liked means being "on." When being valued means being capable, polished, or entertaining. When your worth feels tied to how well you present yourself.

If this is your intention style, you don't communicate to deceive — you communicate to be enough. You share the best version of yourself, you keep things light, you stay competent, and you avoid showing struggle. You want connection, but you fear that your unfiltered self might not be welcomed.

The Performer is not vanity. It is protection.

This chapter is an invitation to understand the story behind your shine — and to learn how to let people see you without the performance.

✿ Why the Performer Emerges

The Performer often develops in environments where:

- praise was tied to achievement
- attention came when you excelled

- emotions were minimized or dismissed
- vulnerability was met with discomfort
- you were expected to be strong, capable, or impressive
- you learned that being "easy" or "entertaining" kept the peace

So you learned to:

- stay upbeat
- stay competent
- stay polished
- stay agreeable
- stay in control of how others see you

These skills helped you feel valued. But they can make authenticity feel risky.

༄ How the Performer Communicates

When the Performer leads, communication often sounds like:

- being upbeat even when you're tired
- sharing accomplishments instead of emotions
- keeping conversations light
- avoiding topics that reveal struggle
- overexplaining to prove you're capable
- using humor to deflect discomfort
- staying composed even when you're hurting

You may notice:

- you rarely ask for help
- you feel pressure to "show up well"
- you downplay your pain
- you fear disappointing others

- you feel responsible for keeping the mood positive
- you struggle to let people see your messier emotions

The Performer communicates to be accepted — not for who you are, but for how well you appear.

৶ The Hidden Need of the Performer

Beneath the polish is a tender, human need:

"I need to feel valued for my real self."

Not the curated version. Not the capable version. Not the entertaining version. The real one.

The Performer is not trying to impress. The Performer is trying to belong.

৶ The Strengths of the Performer

This intention style carries beautiful gifts:

- You bring joy and lightness to conversations.
- You are engaging, charismatic, and thoughtful.
- You uplift others with your energy.
- You are adaptable and socially intuitive.
- You know how to make people feel comfortable.
- You are resourceful and solution-oriented.

When grounded, the Performer becomes a vibrant, inspiring communicator who brings warmth and confidence to every space.

৶ The Challenges of the Performer

When the Performer is overactive, communication can feel:

- surface-level

- emotionally distant
- overly polished
- exhausting
- inauthentic
- lonely

Others may assume you're always okay. They may rely on your strength without realizing you're struggling. They may never see your deeper needs because you've learned to hide them behind competence.

The challenge is not your shine — it's the pressure to maintain it.

Letting Yourself Be Seen Without Performing

You don't need to dim your light. You need to stop hiding behind it.

Here are gentle shifts that help:

- Replace "I'm good!" with "It's been a full week — I'm managing."
- Replace humor with honesty when something hurts.
- Replace overexplaining with simple truth.
- Replace perfection with presence.
- Replace "I've got it" with "I could use some support."

These shifts invite people into your real world — not just your highlight reel.

A Grounding Practice for the Performer

Before responding, ask yourself:

- *Am I sharing my truth or my presentation?*
- *What am I afraid people will think if I'm honest?*
- *What would it feel like to be seen without performing?*
- *What do I need right now that I'm afraid to ask for?*

This practice helps you communicate from authenticity instead of image.

᧒ Closing Thought

The Performer is not here to deceive. It is here to protect the parts of you that once felt unseen.

But you deserve relationships where you don't have to perform to be loved. Where your truth is welcome. Where your imperfections are safe. Where your presence matters more than your presentation.

When you let people see the real you, you create connection that is deep, honest, and liberating.

ᨀ Reflection Prompts

✦ *Self-Reflection*

- When do I feel pressure to "show up well"?
- What emotions do I hide behind humor, competence, or positivity?
- What am I afraid people will think if I'm honest about my struggles?
- What parts of me feel unseen or unacknowledged?

✦ *Connection Reflection*

- Who feels safe enough for me to be real with?
- How do others respond when I drop the performance?
- What small truth could I share this week instead of a polished version?

CHAPTER 7 SUMMARY — THE PERFORMER

- The Performer communicates to be accepted and valued.
- This style forms in environments where worth was tied to achievement.

- Strengths: charisma, adaptability, positivity, resourcefulness.
- Challenges: emotional distance, over-polishing, hidden loneliness.
- Healing comes from sharing truth instead of presentation.

8

The Prover

When certainty becomes your communication style

The Prover shows up when your worth has been questioned. When you've had to justify your decisions, your feelings, or your intelligence. When being misunderstood felt dangerous or humiliating. When clarity became your shield and correctness became your safety.

If this is your intention style, you don't communicate to dominate — you communicate to ensure you're not dismissed. You gather facts, you explain thoroughly, you choose your words carefully, and you work hard to make sure your point is airtight. You want connection, but you fear being misinterpreted, minimized, or made to feel small.

The Prover is not arrogance. It is protection.

This chapter is an invitation to honor the intelligence behind your precision — and to learn how to communicate with confidence without carrying the weight of constant justification.

✿ Why the Prover Emerges

The Prover often develops in environments where:

- your feelings were questioned or invalidated
- you were told you were "too sensitive," "too emotional," or "overreacting"
- you had to defend your choices
- you were blamed for things you didn't do
- you were misunderstood often
- you felt pressure to be competent or perfect

So you learned to:

- gather evidence
- anticipate arguments
- explain everything clearly
- avoid being wrong
- stay emotionally composed
- protect yourself with logic

These skills helped you stay grounded. But they can make vulnerability feel unsafe.

✿ How the Prover Communicates

When the Prover leads, communication often sounds like:

- explaining your reasoning in detail
- clarifying your intentions repeatedly
- correcting misunderstandings quickly
- using logic to stay in control
- avoiding emotional language

- needing conversations to be accurate and fair
- feeling frustrated when others "don't get it"

You may notice:

- you replay conversations to see where the misunderstanding happened
- you feel anxious when things are unclear
- you struggle when others communicate vaguely
- you feel responsible for making sure the truth is known
- you fear being blamed or misrepresented

The Prover communicates to protect your integrity — not to win.

๛ The Hidden Need of the Prover

Beneath the precision is a tender, human need:
"I need to feel understood and respected."
Not for your logic — for your humanity.
The Prover is not trying to be right. The Prover is trying to be seen accurately.

๛ The Strengths of the Prover

This intention style carries powerful gifts:

- You bring clarity to confusing situations.
- You think deeply and communicate thoughtfully.
- You are fair, consistent, and grounded.
- You value truth and integrity.
- You help others see the full picture.
- You are emotionally steady in difficult conversations.

When balanced, the Prover becomes a wise, stabilizing communicator who brings structure and understanding to every space.

ॐ The Challenges of the Prover

When the Prover is overactive, communication can feel:

- rigid
- overly detailed
- emotionally distant
- defensive
- exhausting
- like a debate instead of a dialogue

Others may feel corrected when you're simply clarifying. They may feel dismissed when you're trying to be precise. They may feel overwhelmed when you're trying to be thorough.

The challenge is not your intelligence — it's the pressure to prove it.

ॐ Releasing the Pressure to Prove

You don't need to stop being thoughtful. You need to stop carrying the burden of constant justification.

Here are gentle shifts that help:

- Replace "That's not what I said" with "Let me try saying it another way."
- Replace "Here's why I'm right" with "Here's what I'm trying to express."
- Replace overexplaining with one clear sentence.
- Replace defensiveness with curiosity.
- Replace logic-only responses with small emotional truths.

These shifts create space for connection instead of correction.

⟋ A Grounding Practice for the Prover

Before responding, ask yourself:

- *Am I trying to connect or to be understood perfectly?*
- *What am I afraid will happen if I'm misunderstood?*
- *What emotion is underneath my need to explain?*
- *What would it feel like to trust that my worth is not on trial?*

This practice helps you communicate from confidence instead of fear.

⟋ Closing Thought

The Prover is not here to argue. It is here to protect your dignity.

But you deserve relationships where you don't have to defend your worth. Where your truth is welcome even when it's imperfect. Where your voice is valued without needing evidence. Where connection matters more than correctness.

When you release the pressure to prove, you make room for deeper understanding — the kind that honors both your mind and your heart.

❦ Reflection Prompts

✧ Self-Reflection

- When do I feel the strongest need to explain or justify myself?
- What emotions rise when I feel misunderstood?
- What am I afraid will happen if I'm wrong or unclear?
- What parts of me feel unseen or misinterpreted?

✧ *Connection Reflection*

- How do others respond when I communicate from a place of precision or defensiveness?
- What would help me feel safe enough to express emotion instead of logic?
- What small truth could I share this week without overexplaining?

CHAPTER 8 SUMMARY — THE PROVER

- The Prover communicates to avoid being misunderstood or dismissed.
- This style forms in environments where your worth or truth was questioned.
- Strengths: clarity, fairness, depth, emotional steadiness.
- Challenges: defensiveness, overexplaining, emotional distance.
- Healing comes from trusting that your worth is not on trial.

9

The Peacemaker

When avoiding conflict becomes your communication style

The Peacemaker shows up when conflict feels like danger. When raised voices, tension, or emotional intensity make your body tighten. When you've learned that staying quiet, agreeable, or neutral keeps the peace — even if it costs you your truth.

If this is your intention style, you don't communicate to deceive — you communicate to prevent disruption. You soften your opinions, hold back your needs, and avoid hard conversations because you fear the emotional fallout. You want connection, but you fear conflict will break it.

The Peacemaker is not passivity. It is protection.

This chapter is an invitation to honor the wisdom behind your calm — and to learn how to speak your truth without losing your peace.

᧙ Why the Peacemaker Emerges

The Peacemaker often develops in environments where:

- conflict was unpredictable or explosive
- emotional intensity felt overwhelming

- you were expected to "keep the peace"
- your needs were overshadowed by others' emotions
- you learned that silence prevented chaos
- expressing yourself led to tension or punishment

So you learned to:

- stay neutral
- avoid confrontation
- minimize your needs
- smooth over tension
- keep your emotions quiet
- prioritize harmony over honesty

These skills helped you stay safe. But they can make authenticity feel threatening.

๛ How the Peacemaker Communicates

When the Peacemaker leads, communication often sounds like:

- "It's not a big deal."
- "I don't want to argue."
- "Let's just move on."
- "I'm okay, really."
- "Whatever works for you."

You may notice:

- you shut down when conversations get heated
- you avoid expressing frustration
- you feel overwhelmed by emotional intensity
- you struggle to make decisions when others are involved

- you fear disappointing or upsetting people
- you replay conversations wishing you had spoken up

The Peacemaker communicates to maintain calm — even at the cost of your own clarity.

The Hidden Need of the Peacemaker

Beneath the quiet is a tender, human need:
"I need to feel emotionally safe."
Not safe from danger — safe from overwhelm.
The Peacemaker is not trying to avoid responsibility. The Peacemaker is trying to avoid emotional chaos.

The Strengths of the Peacemaker

This intention style carries beautiful gifts:

- You bring calm to tense situations.
- You are thoughtful, patient, and steady.
- You listen deeply and without judgment.
- You create environments where others feel comfortable.
- You are intuitive about emotional dynamics.
- You value harmony and connection.

When balanced, the Peacemaker becomes a grounding presence — someone who brings peace without losing themselves.

The Challenges of the Peacemaker

When the Peacemaker is overactive, communication can feel:

- unclear

- indirect
- avoidant
- emotionally distant
- resentful beneath the surface
- disconnected from your own needs

Others may assume you're fine when you're not. They may unintentionally overlook your needs because you rarely express them. They may feel confused because your silence hides your truth.

The challenge is not your calm — it's the cost of it.

৶ Finding Your Voice Without Losing Your Peace

You don't need to become confrontational. You need to become honest.
Here are gentle shifts that help:

- Replace "It's fine" with "I do have a preference."
- Replace silence with small truths spoken softly.
- Replace avoidance with curiosity.
- Replace shutting down with "I need a moment to process."
- Replace "I don't want to argue" with "I want to talk about this calmly."

These shifts allow you to stay grounded while still being real.

৶ A Grounding Practice for the Peacemaker

Before responding, ask yourself:

- *Am I staying quiet to keep the peace or because I'm truly okay?*
- *What emotion am I avoiding right now?*
- *What do I need that I'm afraid to express?*
- *What would it feel like to trust that conflict doesn't equal danger?*

This practice helps you speak from courage instead of fear.

☌ Closing Thought

The Peacemaker is not here to silence you. It is here to protect your nervous system.

But you deserve relationships where your truth doesn't disrupt the peace — it deepens it. Where your needs matter. Where your voice is welcome. Where conflict is not a threat, but a pathway to understanding.When you speak honestly, you create connection that is calm, grounded, and real.

☙ Reflection Prompts

✦ *Self-Reflection*

- What emotions or conversations do I avoid most often?
- What does conflict feel like in my body?
- What am I afraid will happen if I express my frustration or needs?
- What truths do I silence to keep the peace?

✦ *Connection Reflection*

- How do others respond when I withdraw or shut down?
- What relationships feel safe enough for me to practice honesty?
- What small truth could I express this week instead of staying silent?

CHAPTER 9 SUMMARY — THE PEACEMAKER

- The Peacemaker communicates to avoid conflict and emotional over-whelm.
- This style forms in environments where tension felt unsafe.
- Strengths: calm, patience, deep listening, emotional intuition.

- Challenges: avoidance, self-silencing, hidden resentment.
- Healing comes from expressing truth gently and trusting that conflict can be safe.

10

The Planner

When control becomes your communication style

The Planner shows up when uncertainty feels unsafe. When not knowing what will happen next makes your body tighten. When structure, preparation, and clarity become your way of staying emotionally steady. When you've learned that the best way to avoid disappointment is to stay ahead of it.

If this is your intention style, you don't communicate to control people — you communicate to control outcomes. You ask detailed questions, you think several steps ahead, you anticipate problems, and you try to prevent surprises. You want connection, but you fear chaos, confusion, or unmet expectations.

The Planner is not rigidity. It is protection.

This chapter is an invitation to honor the wisdom behind your foresight — and to learn how to trust connection more than control.

ᐠ Why the Planner Emerges

The Planner often develops in environments where:

- unpredictability was common
- you had to manage other people's emotions

- responsibility was placed on you early
- mistakes were met with criticism
- you felt safer when things were structured
- you learned to anticipate problems before they happened

So you learned to:

- prepare
- organize
- predict
- manage
- plan
- prevent

These skills helped you stay grounded. But they can make spontaneity feel threatening.

๏ How the Planner Communicates

When the Planner leads, communication often sounds like:

- asking clarifying questions
- needing details before making decisions
- wanting to know the plan ahead of time
- offering solutions quickly
- trying to prevent misunderstandings
- managing logistics even in emotional conversations
- struggling when others are vague or unpredictable

You may notice:

- you feel anxious when things are last-minute
- you get frustrated when others don't think ahead

- you take on responsibility that isn't yours
- you struggle to relax when things feel uncertain
- you replay conversations to analyze what could go wrong
- you feel safer when you're prepared

The Planner communicates to create stability — not to control others.

ꕥ The Hidden Need of the Planner

Beneath the structure is a tender, human need:

"I need to feel secure."

Not secure in the sense of perfection — secure in the sense of predictability, clarity, and emotional steadiness.

The Planner is not trying to micromanage. The Planner is trying to feel safe.

ꕥ The Strengths of the Planner

This intention style carries powerful gifts:

- You bring order to chaos.
- You think ahead in ways others appreciate.
- You are reliable, thoughtful, and prepared.
- You help people feel safe and supported.
- You are excellent at problem-solving.
- You create structure that helps relationships thrive.

When balanced, the Planner becomes a steady, grounding communicator who brings clarity and confidence to every space.

๛ The Challenges of the Planner

When the Planner is overactive, communication can feel:

- rigid
- controlling
- overly structured
- impatient
- anxious
- emotionally distant

Others may feel micromanaged when you're simply trying to help. They may feel pressured when you're trying to prevent problems. They may feel overwhelmed when you're trying to create clarity.

The challenge is not your planning — it's the fear underneath it.

๛ Trusting Connection More Than Control

You don't need to stop planning. You need to stop carrying the emotional weight of every outcome.

Here are gentle shifts that help:

- Replace "What's the plan?" with "What are we hoping for?"
- Replace "Let me handle it" with "How can we share this?"
- Replace "We need to decide now" with "Let's take a moment."
- Replace over-explaining with one clear question.
- Replace managing with collaborating.

These shifts create space for flexibility without sacrificing stability.

๛ A Grounding Practice for the Planner

Before responding, ask yourself:

- *Am I trying to connect or to control the outcome?*
- *What uncertainty is making me uncomfortable right now?*
- *What do I need to feel grounded?*
- *What would it feel like to trust that things can unfold without me managing every detail?*

This practice helps you communicate from presence instead of pressure.

๛ Closing Thought

The Planner is not here to restrict you. It is here to protect you from the unpredictability that once felt overwhelming.

But you deserve relationships where you don't have to manage everything. Where you can rest. Where you can trust. Where connection is built on collaboration, not control.

When you loosen your grip — even slightly — you make room for joy, spontaneity, and deeper intimacy.

๛ Reflection Prompts

✦ Self-Reflection

- What situations make me feel the strongest need to plan or control?
- What emotions rise when things feel uncertain or unstructured?
- What am I afraid will happen if I don't manage the details?
- What responsibilities do I carry that aren't actually mine?

✧ *Connection Reflection*

- How do others respond when I communicate from a place of urgency or structure?
- What would it feel like to collaborate instead of manage?
- What small moment this week could I allow to unfold naturally?

CHAPTER 10 SUMMARY— THE PLANNER

- The Planner communicates to create stability and prevent uncertainty.
- This style forms in environments where unpredictability felt unsafe.
- Strengths: organization, foresight, reliability, problem-solving.
- Challenges: rigidity, over-responsibility, anxiety, control.
- Healing comes from trusting connection more than outcomes.

11

The Processor

The Processor is the intention style that moves slowly, thoughtfully, and intentionally. It is the part of you that needs time to understand what you're feeling before you can express it. The Processor doesn't rush, react, or perform. It pauses. It observes. It thinks. It gathers the pieces before speaking.

This style is not cold or distant — it is careful. It is not disengaged — it is processing. It is not avoiding — it is preparing to respond with clarity.

The Processor is the version of you that wants to get it right, not for approval, but for accuracy. It wants to understand the full picture before stepping into the conversation. It wants to honor the moment by not speaking prematurely.

But here's the challenge: The world often rewards speed, not depth. Many relationships expect immediate responses, not thoughtful ones. And when emotions rise, people often misinterpret silence as disinterest, withdrawal, or rejection.

The Processor is none of these things. It is simply taking time to understand.

This chapter explores how to honor your Processor without disappearing, how to communicate your need for time without shutting down connection, and how to return to presence when overwhelm tries to take over.

The Heart of the Processor: Clarity Over Speed

The Processor values clarity. It wants to understand what's happening inside before responding to what's happening outside.

This looks like:

- Pausing before answering
- Needing space to think
- Feeling overwhelmed by emotional intensity
- Struggling to speak when caught off guard
- Wanting to reflect before responding

The Processor is not indecisive — it is intentional. It is not slow — it is thorough. It is not detached — it is internal.

When honored, the Processor brings depth, wisdom, and emotional steadiness to conversations. When rushed, it shuts down.

How the Processor Shows Up in Communication

1. Silence Before Speech

The Processor often goes quiet before it goes deep. This silence is not avoidance — it is preparation.

2. Internal Overwhelm

When emotions rise too quickly, the Processor may freeze. It needs time to sort through the noise.

3. Thoughtful Responses

When given space, the Processor communicates with clarity, intention, and grounded insight.

4. Delayed Understanding

Sometimes the Processor doesn't know what it feels until hours later — and that's okay.

What the Processor Needs

Time

Not endless time — just enough to breathe, think, and settle.

Space Without Disconnection

The Processor needs room to process, but not abandonment.

Gentle Pace

Fast, intense conversations overwhelm the Processor's nervous system.

Permission to Return Later

The Processor communicates best when it can revisit the conversation with clarity.

How to Support Your Processor in Real Time

1. Name What's Happening

"I need a moment to think." "I'm processing." "I want to respond clearly, not reactively."

Naming it keeps the other person from feeling shut out.

2. Set a Return Time

"I need 20 minutes." "Can we talk about this tonight?" "I'll come back to this after I've had time to think."

This protects connection while honoring your pace.

3. Breathe Before You Speak

A slow breath helps your thoughts settle.

4. Write Before You Talk

Sometimes clarity comes through writing first.

5. Stay Present Even If You're Quiet

You can be silent without disappearing.

When Old Patterns Pull You Away From the Processor

When overwhelmed, the Processor may shift into:

- **Protector** → shutting down to avoid emotional intensity
- **Pleaser** → agreeing quickly to end discomfort
- **Performer** → over-explaining to fill silence
- **Prover** → defending instead of processing
- **Peacemaker** → withdrawing to keep the peace

· **Planner** → trying to control the outcome

Returning to the Processor means slowing down, breathing, and giving yourself permission to think before responding.

Returning to the Processor

The Processor is not a flaw — it is a gift. It brings depth, clarity, and emotional steadiness to your relationships. It helps you respond with intention instead of reacting from overwhelm.

Honoring your Processor means:

· Communicating your need for time
· Staying connected even when quiet
· Returning to the conversation with clarity
· Trusting your internal pace

This is how you build relationships that feel safe, steady, and grounded.

❧ Reflection Prompts

✦ Self-Reflection

· What situations overwhelm me or make it hard to think clearly?
· How does my body feel when I'm processing versus when I'm shutting down?
· What helps me communicate my need for time without withdrawing?
· Which intention style takes over when I feel rushed or pressured?
· What intention do I want to lead with when I return to the conversation?

✦ Connection Reflection

- How do others respond when I communicate my need for time clearly?
- What phrase helps me stay present even when I'm quiet?
- How does the tone of a conversation shift when I return with clarity instead of reacting quickly?
- What boundary supports my Processor during emotionally intense moments?
- What upcoming conversation could I approach with more patience, presence, and internal space?

CHAPTER 11 SUMMARY— THE PROCESSOR

- The Processor communicates best with time, space, and emotional steadiness.
- Silence is not withdrawal — it's preparation for clarity.
- Naming your need for time protects connection and reduces overwhelm.
- Returning later with grounded insight strengthens trust and understanding.
- Honoring your pace creates clearer, calmer, more intentional communication.

III

❧ Part III — The Practice of Intentional Communication

Awareness is powerful, but awareness alone doesn't change our relationships.
Transformation happens in the practice — in the small, everyday moments where we choose presence over reaction, clarity over assumption, and connection over control.

This section is not about speaking perfectly. It's about speaking purposefully.

12

Speak From Your Truth, Not Your Triggers

How to respond instead of react

By now, you've explored all seven intention styles — the Protector, the Pleaser, the Performer, the Prover, the Peacemaker, the Planner, and the Processor. You've seen the wisdom behind each one, the tenderness beneath the patterns, and the ways they shape your communication without your permission.

But awareness is only the beginning.

This chapter is about learning to speak from your truth — the grounded, steady place within you that isn't ruled by fear, habit, or emotional reflex. Your truth is where clarity lives. It's where compassion lives. It's where your real intention lives.

Speaking from your truth doesn't mean you never get triggered. It means you don't let the trigger speak for you.

๑ What It Means to Speak From Your Truth

Speaking from your truth means:

- you pause before reacting
- you choose your intention consciously
- you speak from clarity instead of fear

- you express needs without apology
- you stay connected to yourself even in conflict
- you communicate with honesty, not confusion
- you honor your values instead of your patterns

Your truth is not a personality. It's a posture.

A grounded, steady, emotionally regulated posture that allows you to respond instead of react.

᧿ Why We Speak From Our Triggers Instead of Our Truth

We lose access to our truth when:

- we feel misunderstood
- we feel disrespected
- we feel overwhelmed
- we feel rushed
- we feel unheard
- we feel unsafe
- we feel emotionally flooded

And in those moments, our intention style takes over:

The Protector sharpens. The Pleaser softens. The Performer polishes. The Prover explains. The Peacemaker withdraws. The Planner controls. The Processor shuts down to think.

These patterns are not failures — they are signals. Signals that you've left your truth and entered your trigger.

๛ Returning to Your Truth

You return to your truth through awareness, breath, and choice.

Here's a simple three-step practice:

1. Notice the shift.

Ask yourself: **"Which intention style is trying to take over right now?"**

This is not judgment — it's information.

2. Ground your body.

Slow your breath. Relax your shoulders. Unclench your jaw. Feel your feet on the floor.

Your body is the doorway back to your truth.

3. Choose your intention.

Ask yourself: **"What do I want to create in this moment?"** Connection? Clarity? Understanding? Repair? Honesty?

Your intention becomes your anchor.

๛ Speaking From Your Truth Sounds Like...

"Let me slow down so I can respond clearly." "I want us to understand each other." "Here's what I'm feeling and what I need." "I'm not trying to argue — I'm trying to connect." "Can we take a breath and start again?" "I want to stay grounded while we talk about this."

These phrases shift the emotional tone instantly. They bring you back to yourself. They bring the conversation back to safety.

◌ The Power of the Truth-Centered Pause

The pause is your greatest communication tool.

A pause is not withdrawal. A pause is not avoidance. A pause is not weakness.

A pause is power.

It gives your nervous system time to settle. It gives your intention time to rise. It gives your words time to align with your truth.

The pause is where transformation happens.

◌ Speaking From Your Truth Creates Emotional Safety

When you speak from your truth:

- others feel less defensive
- conversations stay grounded
- misunderstandings decrease
- clarity increases
- connection deepens
- conflict becomes manageable
- your needs become clearer
- your relationships feel safer

Your truth is your most powerful voice.

◌ Closing Thought

You don't have to silence your intention style — you simply have to lead it.

When you speak from your truth, you communicate with wisdom, clarity, and compassion. You become someone who can navigate hard conversations without losing yourself. You become someone who builds emotional safety with your presence alone.

Speaking from your truth is not perfection. It is practice. And every moment gives you another chance to return.

❧ Reflection Prompts

✧ Self-Reflection

- What situations pull me out of my truth most quickly?
- Which intention style takes over when I feel overwhelmed?
- What does my body feel like when I'm grounded versus triggered?
- What intention do I want to lead with more often?

✧ Connection Reflection

- How do others respond when I communicate from a grounded place?
- What phrase or practice helps me return to my truth?
- What conversation this week could I approach from my truth instead of my trigger?

CHAPTER 12 SUMMARY — SPEAK FROM YOUR TRUTH, NOT YOUR TRIGGERS

- Your truth is the grounded place beneath your patterns.
- You lose your truth when you feel unsafe, rushed, or misunderstood.
- Returning to your truth requires awareness, breath, and intention.
- Speaking from your truth creates emotional safety and clarity.
- The pause is your most powerful communication tool.

13

Say What You Mean Without Losing What Matters

Balancing honesty with compassion

Most people think communication is shaped by what they say. But the truth is, communication is shaped just as much — if not more — by how we listen, how we interpret, and how we hold the emotional space between us.

Honesty without compassion becomes harsh. Compassion without honesty becomes unclear. Healthy communication requires both.

Saying what you mean is powerful. Saying it without losing what matters — the relationship, the connection, the emotional safety — is transformational.

This chapter is about learning to express truth in a way that honors both your voice and the person in front of you.

❧ Why Honesty Matters — And Why It's Hard

People don't just want honesty — they want honesty that feels safe.
They want to know:

- your truth won't harm them
- your clarity won't erase their feelings
- your needs won't threaten the relationship

- your boundaries won't punish them
- your voice won't silence theirs

Honesty becomes healing when it is delivered with presence, not pressure.

❧ Honesty vs. Compassion: The False Choice

Many of us were taught that we must choose:

Be honest OR be kind. Speak up OR keep the peace. Tell the truth OR protect the relationship.

But intentional communication requires both.

Honesty without compassion is sharp. Compassion without honesty is vague. Together, they create clarity that feels safe.

❧ How Your Intention Style Shapes Your Honesty

Each intention style has a default way of expressing truth — or avoiding it.

The Protector sharpens the truth. **The Pleaser** softens the truth. **The Performer** polishes the truth. **The Prover** overexplains the truth. **The Peacemaker** avoids the truth. **The Planner** structures the truth. **The Processor** delays the truth until it feels fully formed.

None of these are wrong — they're protective.

But they can blur your message, distort your tone, or disconnect you from what matters most.

Saying what you mean requires leading your intention style instead of letting it lead you.

❧ What It Means to Say What You Mean

Saying what you mean doesn't require:

- harshness
- urgency

- emotional intensity
- defensiveness
- perfection

It requires:

- grounded tone
- clear intention
- simple language
- emotional awareness
- compassion for the listener

Saying what you mean is not about being blunt. It's about being honest without abandoning connection.

❧ What People Are Really Asking For Beneath Their Words

Most people don't speak in needs — they speak in reactions.

Behind:

"Why would you say that?" is often **"I feel hurt."**

Behind:

"You don't care." is often **"I need reassurance."**

Behind:

"Forget it." is often **"I don't feel safe enough to continue."**

Behind:

"You never listen." is often **"I feel invisible."**

Saying what you mean requires listening for the need beneath the reaction — in yourself and in others.

๛ How to Say What You Mean Without Losing What Matters

1. Slow down before you speak

Your truth is clearest when your nervous system is calm.

2. Lead with intention

Ask yourself: **"What do I want to protect — my ego or the relationship?"**

3. Speak simply

One sentence of truth is more powerful than ten sentences of explanation.

4. Name your emotion without blame

"I feel…" not "You made me…"

5. Add compassion to your clarity

"I want to talk about this because I care about us."

6. Stay open after you speak

Honesty is not a monologue — it's an invitation.

๛ Honesty That Heals vs. Honesty That Hurts

Honesty that hurts is reactive, rushed, or rooted in fear. **Honesty that heals** is grounded, thoughtful, and rooted in connection.

Honesty that hurts says: "You're the problem."
Honesty that heals says: "Here's what I'm feeling, and here's what I need."

Honesty that hurts demands. Honesty that heals invites.

๛ The Three Levels of Compassionate Honesty

1. Truth

What you're actually feeling or needing.

2. Tone

How you deliver it.

3. Tenderness

Your awareness of the other person's humanity.

When all three are present, honesty becomes a bridge, not a barrier.

๛ What Compassionate Honesty Is Not

It is not:

- abandoning your needs
- cushioning your truth until it disappears
- absorbing someone else's emotions
- avoiding discomfort
- apologizing for your boundaries

Compassion is not self-erasure. Compassion is clarity with care.

❦ Closing Thought

Saying what you mean is not about being louder — it's about being truer. When you speak with honesty and compassion:

- you reduce confusion
- you strengthen connection
- you create emotional safety
- you honor your needs
- you protect what matters
- you communicate from your center

Honesty is a gift. Compassion is the wrapping. Together, they make your truth easier to receive.

❧ Reflection Prompts

✧ Self-Reflection

- What do I usually listen for — understanding, approval, threats, mistakes, tension, or clarity?
- What emotions make it hardest for me to speak honestly?
- What does my body do when I'm speaking from fear instead of compassion?
- What helps me stay grounded while expressing something difficult?

✧ Connection Reflection

- How do others respond when I speak with honesty and care?
- What phrase could I use more often to show I'm balancing truth with compassion?
- What conversation this week could benefit from clearer, kinder honesty?

CHAPTER 13 SUMMARY — SAY WHAT YOU MEAN WITHOUT LOSING WHAT MATTERS

- Honesty is powerful when paired with compassion.
- Your intention style shapes how you express truth.
- Speak simply, calmly, and with emotional awareness.
- Compassion does not require self-erasure.
- Truth + tone + tenderness = communication that connects.

14

Listening for What's Not Being Said

How to hear emotions, not just words

Most people believe communication is shaped by what they say. But the truth is, communication is shaped just as much — if not more — by what they *don't* say.

People rarely speak in pure emotion. They speak in reactions, habits, and protective patterns. They speak through tone, silence, body language, and unfinished sentences.

Listening for what's not being said is the art of hearing beneath the surface — the emotion, the need, the fear, the longing, the story behind the words.

This chapter is about learning to listen in a way that reveals truth, deepens connection, and creates emotional safety for both people.

൮ Why Listening for the Unspoken Matters

People don't just want to be heard — they want to be *felt*.

They want to know:

- their emotions are seen
- their needs are understood
- their experience is valid
- their silence is noticed

- their heart is safe

When someone feels emotionally understood, their nervous system relaxes. Their defensiveness softens. Their communication becomes clearer. Their truth becomes easier to share.

Listening for the unspoken is how you create emotional safety.

ᵒᵖ Words Are Only Part of the Story

Hearing is automatic. Listening is intentional. But listening for what's not being said is intuitive.

It means paying attention to:

- tone
- pace
- pauses
- body language
- shifts in energy
- what they emphasize
- what they avoid
- what they repeat
- what they rush through
- what they can't say yet

People reveal more in their hesitation than in their explanation.

ᵒᵖ What People Are Really Saying Beneath Their Words

Most people don't speak in needs — they speak in reactions.

Behind:

"I'm fine." is often **"I don't feel safe enough to open up."**

Behind:

"Whatever." is often **"I feel dismissed."**

Behind:

"You don't get it." is often **"I feel alone in this."**

Behind:

"It's not a big deal." is often **"It actually matters a lot, but I'm scared to say it."**

Behind:

Silence is often **"I'm overwhelmed and trying to protect myself."**

Listening for the unspoken means listening for the emotion, not just the expression.

How Your Intention Style Shapes What You Hear

Each intention style listens through its own filter:

The Protector listens for threats. **The Pleaser** listens for disappointment. **The Performer** listens for approval. **The Prover** listens for inaccuracies. **The Peacemaker** listens for tension. **The Planner** listens for problems to solve. **The Processor** listens for clarity and time to think.

When you listen from your intention style, you hear through your fear. When you listen from your center, you hear through your presence.

Listening for What's Not Being Said Requires Presence

Listening for the unspoken means:

- you slow down
- you breathe
- you stay curious
- you let silence speak
- you reflect back what you sense
- you ask gentle clarifying questions
- you validate the emotion beneath the words

It sounds like:

"I hear what you're saying, and I'm also sensing something underneath." "It seems like this feels heavier than the words you're using." "I want to understand what this really means for you." "Take your time — I'm here." "What feels hardest to say right now?"

These phrases open the emotional door.

ꝏ The Three Layers of Unspoken Communication

1. The Words

What they say.

2. The Emotion

What they feel.

3. The Need

What they're longing for.

When you listen at all three levels, you create connection that feels safe, deep, and honest.

ꝏ What Listening for the Unspoken Is Not

It is not:

- assuming you know everything
- diagnosing someone's emotions
- interrupting their process
- absorbing their feelings
- fixing the problem immediately
- forcing them to open up

Listening for the unspoken is not about reading minds. It's about reading the moment.

ꝏ Closing Thought

Listening for what's not being said is one of the most powerful forms of emotional presence. It turns conversations into connection. It turns silence into understanding. It turns defensiveness into safety. It turns distance into closeness.

When you listen with your presence, not your patterns, you become someone others feel safe revealing their truth to — even the parts they struggle to say out loud.

✿ Reflection Prompts

✧ Self-Reflection

- What do I usually listen for — emotion, approval, threats, mistakes, tension, or clarity?
- What emotions make it hardest for me to hear beneath the words?
- What does my body do when I'm listening from fear instead of presence?
- What helps me stay grounded while someone else is expressing them-selves?

✧ Connection Reflection

- How do others respond when I listen for emotion instead of reacting to words?
- What phrase could I use more often to show I'm listening beneath the surface?
- What conversation this week could benefit from deeper, more intuitive listening?

CHAPTER 14 SUMMARY — LISTENING FOR WHAT'S NOT BEING SAID
- Words are only part of the story.
- People reveal truth through tone, silence, and emotion.
- Your intention style shapes what you hear.
- Listening for the unspoken creates emotional safety.
- Listen for the words, the emotion, and the need.

15

Repairing Conversations That Went Wrong

Scripts, tools, and practices for reconnection

Every relationship — no matter how loving, intentional, or emotionally mature — will experience moments of rupture. Words get sharp. Feelings get hurt. Assumptions get made. Patterns take over. Silence grows heavy. Distance forms.

Rupture is not a sign of failure. Rupture is a sign of humanity.

What matters is not whether conflict happens — but how you repair.

Repair is the process of returning to connection after disconnection. It is the bridge between "what happened" and "what we want to build next." It is the practice that turns conflict into clarity, and misunderstanding into deeper understanding.

This chapter gives you the scripts, tools, and practices that help you repair conversations that went wrong — gently, intentionally, and with emotional safety at the center.

๛ Why Repair Matters

Repair is how relationships stay strong. It communicates:

- "You matter more than the moment."
- "Our connection is worth returning to."

- "We can do this differently."
- "We're on the same team."

Repair reduces resentment. Repair restores trust. Repair deepens intimacy. Repair teaches your nervous system that conflict is survivable.

Without repair, small ruptures become emotional distance. With repair, ruptures become opportunities for growth.

๙ How Intention Styles Complicate Repair

Each intention style has a predictable way of responding after a conversation goes wrong:

The Protector shuts down or gets defensive. **The Pleaser** apologizes too quickly to avoid tension. **The Performer** tries to fix everything immediately. **The Prover** replays the argument to prove their point. **The Peacemaker** avoids the conversation altogether. **The Planner** tries to control how the repair should go. **The Processor** needs time but doesn't always communicate that.

Understanding your style helps you repair with clarity instead of confusion.

๙ The Three Phases of Repair

Repair is not one moment — it's a process.

1. Regulation

You calm your body so you can return with clarity.

2. Reflection

You understand what happened inside you.

3. Reconnection

You return to the conversation with intention.

Let's walk through each one.

ꙮ Phase 1: Regulation — Before You Try to Repair

You cannot repair from a triggered state. You can only repair from your center.

Regulation looks like:

- stepping away briefly
- breathing slowly
- grounding your body
- naming your emotion
- noticing your intention style
- choosing your intention

A regulated body creates a regulated conversation.

ꙮ Phase 2: Reflection — Understanding What Happened

Ask yourself:

- What was I feeling?
- What was I needing?
- What intention style took over?
- What was I trying to protect?
- What do I want to repair?

Reflection turns reactivity into responsibility.

๑ Phase 3: Reconnection — Returning With Intention

Reconnection is not about blame. It's about clarity, compassion, and accountability.

It sounds like:

- "I want to repair what happened."
- "I care about us, and I want to talk about this."
- "Can we try again with a calmer tone?"
- "I want to understand your experience too."

Reconnection is the moment you choose the relationship over the rupture.

๑ Scripts for Repairing Conversations That Went Wrong

Here are grounded, emotionally safe scripts you can use in real life.

If you reacted too quickly

"Earlier, I reacted from my trigger, not my truth. I want to try again."

If your tone was sharp

"My tone didn't reflect how much I care. I'm sorry. Can we reset?"

If you shut down

"I went quiet because I felt overwhelmed. I'm ready to talk now."

If you said something you regret

"I said that from frustration, not intention. I want to repair that."

If you misunderstood

"I think I misheard you earlier. Can you help me understand what you meant?"

If you need to revisit the conversation

"I've had time to think, and I'd like to talk about what happened."

If you want to reconnect without talking yet

"I'm here. I care. I'm not ready to talk, but I'm not going anywhere."

❧ Tools for Repair

1. The Reset Phrase

A simple phrase that signals a fresh start.
   "Can we reset and try again?"

2. The 10-Minute Pause

Step away briefly, then return with intention.
   "Let's take ten minutes and come back to this."

3. The "I + I" Formula

Impact + Intention
   "I see the impact of what I said, and I want you to know my intention."

4. The Repair Question

"What would help you feel understood right now?"

5. The Shared Truth

"We both want to feel heard and connected."
   This shifts the conversation from "me vs. you" to "us together."

๛ practices for Reconnection

practices help your nervous system trust the repair process.

1. The Hand on Heart Pause

Both people place a hand on their chest and breathe together.

2. The "Try Again" Ritual

One person says, "Can we try that again?" The other responds, "Yes, let's try again."

3. The Evening Reset

A nightly practice: "Is there anything we need to repair before we rest?"

4. The Gratitude Bridge

End the repair with one sentence of appreciation.
   "Thank you for staying in this with me."

⚯ How Each Intention Style Can Practice Repair

Protector: Soften your tone before you speak.

Pleaser: Repair without over-apologizing.

Performer: You don't have to fix everything — just be present.

Prover: Repair without re-arguing the details.

Peacemaker: Stay in the conversation instead of disappearing.

Planner: Let the repair unfold naturally, not perfectly.

Processor: Communicate your need for time, then return.

Repair is not about perfection — it's about presence.

⚯ Closing Thought

Rupture is inevitable. Repair is intentional.

When you repair with clarity, compassion, and courage:

- connection deepens
- trust strengthens
- resentment dissolves
- communication becomes safer
- the relationship becomes more resilient

Repair is not about fixing the past — it's about building the future.

⚘ Reflection Prompts

✧ Self-Reflection

- What intention style shows up most strongly after a rupture?
- What makes it hardest for me to initiate repair?
- What helps me regulate before returning to the conversation?
- What repair script feels most natural for me to use?

✧ Connection Reflection

- How do others respond when I initiate repair calmly?
- What practice or phrase could help us reconnect more easily?
- What conversation this week might benefit from a gentle repair?

CHAPTER 15 SUMMARY — REPAIRING CONVERSATIONS THAT WENT WRONG

- Rupture is human; repair is intentional.
- Each intention style has a predictable repair pattern.
- Regulation → Reflection → Reconnection is the repair pathway.
- Scripts and practices make repair easier and safer.
- Repair deepens trust, connection, and emotional resilience.

16

Boundaries That Build Connection

How to honor yourself without harming the relationship

Most people think boundaries push people away. But healthy boundaries do the opposite — they bring people closer.

Boundaries are not walls. Boundaries are not punishments. Boundaries are not ultimatums.

Boundaries are clarity. Boundaries are honesty. Boundaries are emotional safety in action.

A boundary is simply the line where your responsibility ends and someone else's begins. It is the space where your needs, values, and emotional well-being are honored — without harming the relationship.

This chapter is about learning to set boundaries that strengthen connection rather than strain it. Boundaries that protect your peace *and* protect the relationship. Boundaries that honor your truth without abandoning compassion.

⚘ What Boundaries Really Are

Boundaries are not about controlling others. They are about guiding yourself.

A boundary says:

- "This is what I can offer."
- "This is what I cannot continue doing."

- "This is what I need to feel safe."
- "This is how I want to be treated."
- "This is what supports my well-being."

Boundaries are not demands. They are declarations of self-respect.

๛ Why Boundaries Feel Hard

Boundaries feel difficult because they activate our intention styles:

The Pleaser fears disappointing others. **The Peacemaker** fears conflict. **The Performer** fears looking difficult. **The Prover** fears being misunderstood. **The Protector** fears being vulnerable. **The Planner** fears losing control. **The Processor** fears being rushed into clarity.

Each style has a reason for hesitating. Each style learned to survive by staying small, agreeable, or silent.

But boundaries are not a threat to connection — they are the foundation of healthy connection.

๛ Boundaries That Build Connection vs. Boundaries That Break It

Boundaries that break connection are reactive, rigid, or rooted in fear. They sound like:

- "I'm done."
- "Don't ever do that again."
- "If you loved me, you would..."
- "I'm not dealing with this."

Boundaries that build connection are grounded, clear, and compassionate. They sound like:

- "I want to keep talking, but not in this tone."

- "I need a moment to think before we continue."
- "I care about us, so I need to be honest about what's not working."
- "I want to stay connected, and this is what I need to do that."

Boundaries that build connection protect the relationship, not punish it.

๛ The Three Types of Boundaries

1. Time Boundaries

Protecting your energy and capacity.

"I can talk about this tonight, not right now." "I need a few hours to recharge."

2. Emotional Boundaries

Protecting your internal world.

"I'm not comfortable being spoken to that way." "I need you to lower your voice so I can stay present."

3. Relational Boundaries

Protecting the connection itself.

"I want to stay close, so I need us to communicate differently." "I need honesty between us to feel safe."

᠀ How Each Intention Style Can Practice Healthy Boundaries

Protector: Practice softening your delivery so the boundary doesn't become a barrier.

Pleaser: Practice saying one clear sentence without cushioning it.

Performer: Practice setting boundaries without overexplaining.

Prover: Practice stating the boundary without defending it.

Peacemaker: Practice staying in the conversation instead of disappearing.

Planner: Practice allowing the boundary to evolve instead of controlling every detail.

Processor: Practice communicating your need for time before withdrawing.

Boundaries are not about changing who you are — they're about leading your intention style with clarity.

᠀ How to Set a Boundary Without Harming the Relationship

1. Start with your intention

"What do I want to protect — my peace or my ego?"

2. Speak simply

One sentence is enough.

3. Use "I" language

"I need…" "I'm not available for…" "I can continue this conversation when…"

4. Stay grounded

Your tone matters more than your words.

5. Offer a path forward

Boundaries are not the end of connection — they are the guide back to it.

⚘ Scripts for Boundaries That Build Connection

When you need space

"I want to keep talking, and I need a moment to gather my thoughts."

When the tone becomes harmful

"I care about us, and I can't stay in this conversation if we're yelling."

When you feel overwhelmed

"I'm feeling overloaded. I need a pause so I can respond clearly."

When someone crosses a line

"I'm not comfortable with that. Here's what I need instead."

When you need clarity

"I want to understand you. Can we slow down so I can take this in?"

When you need emotional safety

"I want to stay connected, and I need us to speak respectfully."
   Boundaries are clearest when they are calm, simple, and compassionate.

℘ practices for Boundary Practice

1. The Centering Breath

One slow inhale before speaking your boundary.

2. The "One Sentence" Rule

State your boundary in one clear sentence before adding anything else.

3. The Return Ritual

"I'm stepping away to regulate. I will come back."

4. The Connection Anchor

"I'm setting this boundary because I care about us."
   These practices help your nervous system trust the process.

℘ Closing Thought

Boundaries are not barriers — they are bridges.
   They protect your peace. They protect your truth. They protect your relationships.
   When you set boundaries with clarity and compassion:

- you honor yourself
- you strengthen connection

- you reduce resentment
- you create emotional safety
- you communicate from your center

Boundaries are not the end of closeness — they are the beginning of healthy closeness.

🌿 Reflection Prompts

✧ Self-Reflection

- What fears make it hardest for me to set boundaries?
- Which intention style takes over when I avoid or overcorrect boundaries?
- What boundary have I been softening, delaying, or ignoring?
- What does my body feel like when I honor my boundary versus when I abandon it?

✧ Connection Reflection

- How do others respond when I set boundaries calmly and clearly?
- What phrase or ritual helps me communicate boundaries with compassion?
- What relationship in my life would benefit from a gentle, honest boundary this week?

CHAPTER 16 SUMMARY— BOUNDARIES THAT BUILD CONNECTION

- Boundaries protect connection, not threaten it.
- Each intention style struggles with boundaries differently.
- Clear, compassionate boundaries create emotional safety.
- One sentence is often enough.
- Boundaries honor you *and* strengthen the relationship.

IV

🌿 Part IV — Intentional Communication in Real Life

*It's one thing to understand communication in theory. It's
another to practice it in the moments that matter most.
Real life is where our intention gets tested — in the kitchen, in the
car, in the middle of a disagreement, in a meeting that catches us
off guard, in a conversation we didn't want to have, or in a
moment when someone we love needs more from us than we feel
ready to give.
This is where communication becomes more than a skill. It
becomes a choice.*

17

Intentional Communication In Marriage & Partnership

Speaking with love, clarity, and emotional safety

Marriage and partnership are the places where your intention styles show up the loudest — not because something is wrong, but because partnership is where you are most seen, most vulnerable, and most emotionally invested.

Partnership is where your patterns were formed. Partnership is where your patterns are revealed. Partnership is where your patterns can be transformed.

Speaking with love, clarity, and emotional safety is not about perfection. It's about presence. It's about intention. It's about choosing connection even when the conversation is hard.

This chapter explores how to communicate in ways that honor both people — your truth, your partner's truth, and the relationship you're building together.

❧ Why Partnership Activates Your Intention Styles

Partnership is the most intimate mirror you will ever stand in front of. It reflects:

- your fears

- your hopes
- your wounds
- your habits
- your longing for connection

And because of that, your intention styles rise quickly:

The Protector reacts to stay safe. **The Pleaser** softens to keep peace. **The Performer** polishes to avoid disappointment. **The Prover** explains to feel understood. **The Peacemaker** withdraws to avoid conflict. **The Planner** controls to prevent uncertainty. **The Processor** pauses to gather clarity.

None of these responses are wrong — they are protective. But they can create distance if they lead the conversation.

Partnership requires learning to lead with your center, not your pattern.

᧞ Love Needs Clarity

Love without clarity becomes confusing. Clarity without love becomes cold.

Healthy partnership requires both.

Clarity says: "This is what I feel." "This is what I need." "This is what matters to me."

Love says: "I'm sharing this because I care about us." "I want to stay connected while we talk." "I'm here with you, not against you."

When clarity and love work together, emotional safety grows.

᧞ What Emotional Safety Looks Like in Partnership

Emotional safety is not the absence of conflict. It is the presence of:

- honesty
- gentleness
- curiosity
- repair
- boundaries

- shared responsibility
- mutual respect

Emotional safety is created when both people feel:

- free to speak
- free to feel
- free to pause
- free to be imperfect
- free to return and repair

Safety is not a moment — it's a practice.

൙ How Each Intention Style Communicates in Partnership

Understanding your style helps you communicate with compassion instead of confusion.

Protector: Needs tone softness and reassurance of safety.

Pleaser: Needs permission to express needs without guilt.

Performer: Needs acceptance without performance.

Prover: Needs to feel heard before moving forward.

Peacemaker: Needs gentle pacing and emotional calm.

Planner: Needs clarity and shared responsibility.

Processor: Needs time and space without pressure.

Partnership becomes easier when you honor each other's communication needs.

൙ Speaking With Love in Hard Moments

Speaking with love doesn't mean avoiding truth. It means delivering truth with tenderness.

It sounds like:

- "I want to talk about this because I care about us."
- "I'm feeling something important, and I want to share it gently."
- "I'm not trying to argue — I'm trying to connect."
- "Can we slow down so we can hear each other better?"
- "I want to understand your experience too."

Love is not softness — it is steadiness.

✎ Speaking With Clarity in Hard Moments

Clarity is not harshness. Clarity is honesty with intention.

It sounds like:

- "Here's what I'm feeling."
- "Here's what I need."
- "Here's what I'm asking for."
- "Here's what's not working for me."
- "Here's what would help me feel safer."

Clarity is the foundation of trust.

✎ Speaking With Emotional Safety in Hard Moments

Emotional safety is created through:

- tone
- pacing
- presence
- curiosity
- repair
- boundaries

It sounds like:

- "I'm here. I'm listening."
- "Take your time — I'm not rushing you."
- "I want to understand, not defend."
- "Let's pause and come back with clearer hearts."

Safety is the soil where connection grows.

๛ Tools for Healthy Partnership Communication

1. The "We" Shift

Move from "me vs. you" to "us together."
  "We're both trying to feel understood." "We're on the same team."

2. The Tone Reset

A simple phrase that resets the emotional temperature.
  "Let's slow down and try again."

3. The 10-Minute Pause

Step away briefly, then return with intention.
  "I need a moment to regulate. I will come back."

4. The Clarity Formula

Emotion → Need → Request.
  "I'm feeling overwhelmed. I need a pause. Can we revisit this tonight?"

5. The Repair Ritual

End difficult conversations with connection.
"Thank you for staying in this with me."

๛ How to Stay Connected During Conflict

Connection is not agreement — it is presence.
You stay connected by:

- softening your tone
- slowing your pace
- naming your intention
- validating your partner's feelings
- asking clarifying questions
- returning to repair
- choosing curiosity over defense

Connection is a choice you make again and again.

๛ Closing Thought

Marriage and partnership are not built on perfect communication — they are built on intentional communication.
When you speak with love, clarity, and emotional safety:

- conflict becomes manageable
- trust becomes stronger
- intimacy becomes deeper
- repair becomes easier
- connection becomes more resilient

Partnership is not about avoiding hard conversations — it's about learning to have them with tenderness, truth, and intention.

This is how you build a relationship that feels safe, steady, and sacred.

❧ Reflection Prompts

✧ Self-Reflection

- Which intention style shows up most strongly in my partnership?
- What makes it hardest for me to speak with clarity and love?
- What helps me stay grounded during difficult conversations?
- What truth have I been holding back that needs gentle expression?

✧ Connection Reflection

- How does my partner respond when I speak with emotional safety?
- What phrase or ritual could help us communicate more intentionally?
- What conversation this week could benefit from more love, clarity, and presence?

CHAPTER 17 SUMMARY — IN MARRIAGE & PARTNERSHIP
- Partnership activates your intention styles.
- Love needs clarity; clarity needs love.
- Emotional safety is created through tone, pacing, and presence.
- Each intention style has unique communication needs.
- Speak with tenderness, truth, and intention.

18

Intentional Communication In Parenting

Raising emotionally grounded children through intentional language

Parenting is one of the most powerful places where communication becomes legacy. Your words become their inner voice. Your tone becomes their sense of safety. Your presence becomes their model for connection.

Children don't need perfect parents — they need present ones. Parents who speak with intention. Parents who repair when they miss the mark. Parents who model emotional safety, not emotional suppression.

This chapter explores how to use intentional language to raise children who feel seen, safe, and supported — children who grow into emotionally grounded adults.

๛ Why Parenting Activates Your Intention Styles

Parenting touches every tender part of you — your hopes, your fears, your childhood wounds, your longing to get it right. Because of that, your intention styles rise quickly:

The Protector becomes strict or reactive. **The Pleaser** overaccommodates to avoid conflict. **The Performer** tries to be the "perfect parent." **The Prover** overexplains or lectures. **The Peacemaker** avoids hard conversations. **The Planner** tries to control every outcome. **The Processor** needs time but feels pressured to respond immediately.

None of these responses make you a bad parent — they make you a human parent.

Intentional parenting is not about eliminating your patterns. It's about leading them with awareness.

Children Don't Need Perfection — They Need Regulation

Children learn emotional regulation from your nervous system, not your words.

When you:

- slow down
- breathe
- soften your tone
- name your feelings
- repair when needed

...you teach them how to do the same.

Your regulation becomes their roadmap.

Intentional Language Builds Emotional Safety

Intentional language is not about being soft — it's about being clear, calm, and connected.

It sounds like:

- "I'm here."
- "You're safe."
- "Your feelings make sense."
- "Let's figure this out together."
- "I'm not upset with you — I'm helping you."

Children thrive when they feel emotionally safe enough to express themselves without fear of punishment, shame, or rejection.

❧ What Children Are Really Saying Beneath Their Behavior

Children rarely say what they feel — they show it.

Behind:

"I don't want to!" is often **"I feel overwhelmed."**

Behind:

"Go away!" is often **"I'm scared you're upset with me."**

Behind:

Tantrums is often **"My body is overloaded and I don't know what to do."**

Behind:

Silence is often **"I don't have the words yet."**

Intentional parenting listens beneath the behavior.

❧ How Each Intention Style Can Support Parenting

Protector: Practice softening your tone before correcting.

Pleaser: Practice setting boundaries without guilt.

Performer: Practice letting go of perfection and embracing presence.

Prover: Practice shorter explanations and more connection.

Peacemaker: Practice staying in the moment instead of avoiding conflict.

Planner: Practice flexibility when things don't go as expected.

Processor: Practice saying, "I need a moment to think," instead of shutting down.

Your intention style can become a strength when led with awareness.

⚛ Scripts for Emotionally Grounded Parenting

When your child is overwhelmed

"I see your big feelings. I'm right here with you."

When you need to correct behavior

"I love you. I'm helping you learn."

When you need a moment to regulate

"I'm feeling overwhelmed. I'm going to take a breath and come right back."

When your child makes a mistake

"Mistakes help us grow. Let's figure out what to do next."

When your child shuts down

"It's okay to take your time. I'm here when you're ready."

When you need to set a boundary

"I won't let you speak to me that way. Let's try again with kinder words."
Intentional language teaches emotional intelligence without shame.

⚛ Practices That Build Emotional Grounding

1. The "Name It to Tame It" Ritual

Help your child name their feelings. "You're feeling frustrated. That makes sense."

2. The "Try Again" Ritual

A gentle reset. "Let's try that again with a calmer voice."

3. The "Pause Together" Ritual

Both of you take one slow breath before responding.

4. The "Repair Hug"

After conflict: "I'm sorry for my tone. I love you. We're okay."

5. The "Daily Check-In"

"What was one feeling you had today?"

These practices become emotional anchors.

๛ Teaching Children to Use Their Own Intention Styles

Children have intention styles too — and they often mirror yours.

Help them learn:

Protector: "How can we calm your body before you respond?"

Pleaser: "It's okay to say what you need."

Performer: "You don't have to get it perfect."

Prover: "You don't have to explain everything right now."

Peacemaker: "It's okay to feel upset — you don't have to hide it."

Planner: "Let's practice being flexible together."

Processor: "You can take your time. I'll wait."

This is how emotional grounding becomes generational.

⚘ Closing Thought

Parenting with intention is not about raising perfect children — it's about raising emotionally grounded ones.

Children who know:

- their feelings matter
- their voice matters
- their boundaries matter
- their mistakes don't define them
- their parents are safe places
- their home is a training ground for emotional intelligence

When you speak with intention, you give your children a gift they will carry for life — a voice that is grounded, compassionate, and clear.

This is how you build a legacy of emotional safety.

✾ Reflection Prompts

✧ Self-Reflection

- Which intention style shows up most in my parenting?
- What makes it hardest for me to stay regulated with my child?
- What language did I grow up hearing that I want to do differently?
- What helps me return to presence when I feel overwhelmed?

✧ Connection Reflection

- How does my child respond when I speak calmly and clearly?
- What phrase or ritual helps us reconnect after conflict?

· What moment this week could benefit from more intentional language?

CHAPTER 18 SUMMARY — IN PARENTING
- Children learn emotional regulation from your presence, not your perfection.
- Behavior is communication — listen beneath the surface.
- Each intention style shapes how you parent.
- Intentional language builds emotional safety and connection.
- Practices and repair create grounded, resilient children.

19

Intentional Communication In Leadership & Community

Creating cultures of trust, clarity, and compassion

Leadership is not a title — it's a tone. Community is not a group — it's a culture. And communication is not just what you say — it's what people feel when they're with you.

Whether you lead a team, a classroom, a ministry, a family, or a community space, your presence shapes the emotional climate. Your intention styles influence how people experience you. Your clarity becomes their clarity. Your compassion becomes their safety.

This chapter explores how to lead and build community with intention — creating environments where people feel seen, valued, and emotionally grounded.

๛ Leadership Begins With Emotional Safety

People do their best work — and become their best selves — when they feel safe.

Emotional safety in leadership means:

- people can speak honestly

- mistakes are met with curiosity, not shame
- boundaries are respected
- conflict is navigated with clarity
- feedback is delivered with compassion
- everyone feels like they belong

Safety is not softness — it is structure. Safety is not permissiveness — it is presence.

When people feel safe, they contribute more freely, collaborate more openly, and trust more deeply.

How Intention Styles Show Up in Leadership

Every leader has an intention style that rises under pressure:

The Protector becomes authoritative or reactive. **The Pleaser** avoids hard conversations. **The Performer** overworks to maintain image. **The Prover** overexplains or becomes rigid. **The Peacemaker** avoids conflict or tension. **The Planner** micromanages or overcontrols. **The Processor** withdraws to think but doesn't communicate the pause.

These patterns don't make you a bad leader — they make you a human one.

Leadership becomes powerful when you lead your intention style instead of letting it lead you.

Clarity Is a Leadership Superpower

Clarity is kindness in leadership.

Clarity creates:

- aligned expectations
- reduced confusion
- smoother collaboration
- healthier boundaries
- more confident teams

Clarity sounds like:

- "Here's what success looks like."
- "Here's what I need from you."
- "Here's what you can expect from me."
- "Here's the purpose behind this decision."

Clarity is not control — it is communication.

ꝏ Compassion Is the Heart of Community

Compassion is not lowering standards — it is raising humanity.
   Compassion in leadership looks like:

- listening without defensiveness
- acknowledging emotions
- offering support without rescuing
- giving feedback without shame
- honoring people's lived experiences

Compassion creates belonging. Belonging creates commitment. Commitment creates community.

ꝏ What People Are Really Asking For in Community Spaces

People rarely say what they need directly. They express it through behavior, tone, and participation.
   Behind:
   "I'm fine." is often **"I don't feel safe enough to share."**
   Behind:
   Silence in meetings is often **"I'm afraid of being judged."**
   Behind:

Over-involvement is often **"I'm trying to prove my value."**
Behind:
Withdrawal is often **"I don't feel seen or included."**
Intentional leadership listens beneath the surface.

๛ How to Lead With Trust, Clarity, and Compassion

1. Lead With Transparency

People trust what they understand.

2. Communicate Expectations Clearly

Ambiguity creates anxiety.

3. Model Emotional Regulation

Your calm becomes the room's calm.

4. Invite Voices, Don't Dominate Them

Leadership is shared space, not spotlight.

5. Repair When Needed

Leaders who repair build cultures that heal.

6. Honor Boundaries

Respect creates safety.

7. Celebrate Often

Recognition builds connection.

๛ Scripts for Intentional Leadership & Community Building

When giving feedback

"I'm sharing this because I believe in your growth, not because something is wrong with you."

When addressing conflict

"I want us to understand each other, not blame each other."

When someone feels unheard

"Your perspective matters. Tell me more."

When setting boundaries

"I want to support you well, and here's what I can realistically offer."

When acknowledging emotions

"It makes sense that you feel that way. Thank you for sharing it."

When repairing as a leader

"My tone didn't reflect my intention. I'd like to try again."
These scripts create cultures where people feel valued, not managed.

ॐ practices That Strengthen Community

1. The Check-In Circle

One feeling word before starting a meeting.

2. The "We Before Me" Reminder

"We're on the same team."

3. The Pause & Reset

"Let's slow down and try again."

4. The Appreciation Moment

End gatherings with one sentence of gratitude.

5. The Open Door Ritual

"I'm available if you need clarity or support."
practices turn intention into culture.

ॐ How Each Intention Style Can Lead Well

Protector: Lead with strength *and* softness.
Pleaser: Lead with kindness *and* boundaries.
Performer: Lead with excellence *and* authenticity.

Prover: Lead with clarity *and* flexibility.

Peacemaker: Lead with harmony *and* honesty.

Planner: Lead with structure *and* adaptability.

Processor: Lead with thoughtfulness *and* communication.

Every style has leadership strengths — when guided by intention.

๛ Closing Thought

Leadership and community are not built on charisma — they are built on communication.

When you lead with trust, clarity, and compassion:

- people feel safe
- people feel valued
- people feel connected
- people feel empowered
- people feel like they belong

This is how you build cultures that last. This is how you create communities that heal. This is how you lead with intention, not instinct.

Your leadership becomes legacy

๛ Reflection Prompts

✧ Self-Reflection

- Which intention style shows up most in my leadership?
- What makes it hardest for me to communicate clearly under pressure?
- What helps me stay grounded when leading others?
- What kind of culture do I want to create around me?

✧ Connection Reflection

- How do others respond when I lead with compassion and clarity?
- What phrase or ritual could strengthen trust in my community?
- What leadership moment this week could benefit from more intention?

CHAPTER 19 SUMMARY — IN LEADERSHIP & COMMUNITY
- Leadership is a tone; community is a culture.
- Emotional safety is the foundation of trust.
- Each intention style shapes how you lead.
- Clarity + compassion = connection.
- practices and intentional language create cultures that last.

20

Intentional Communication In Hard Conversations

Navigating conflict, disappointment, and emotional intensity

Hard conversations are unavoidable. They arrive when expectations collide, when emotions rise, when boundaries are crossed, when needs go unmet, when misunderstandings grow, or when silence has stretched too long.

Hard conversations are not a sign that something is broken — they are a sign that something matters.

This chapter is about learning to navigate conflict, disappointment, and emotional intensity with intention. Not with fear. Not with avoidance. Not with defensiveness. But with grounded presence, emotional clarity, and compassion for both yourself and the other person.

᧬ Why Hard Conversations Feel So Hard

Hard conversations activate the parts of us that want to protect, perform, please, or withdraw. They stir up:

- fear of conflict
- fear of hurting someone

- fear of being misunderstood
- fear of being rejected
- fear of losing connection
- fear of being seen too deeply

And because of that, our intention styles rise quickly:

The Protector becomes sharp or reactive. **The Pleaser** softens or avoids. **The Performer** tries to get it "right." **The Prover** explains or defends. **The Peacemaker** shuts down or disappears. **The Planner** tries to control the outcome. **The Processor** freezes or needs time to think.

Hard conversations feel hard because they touch the places where we feel most vulnerable.

Hard Conversations Are Not About Winning — They're About Understanding

The goal is not:

- to win
- to convince
- to prove
- to defend
- to fix
- to control

The goal is:

- clarity
- connection
- understanding
- repair
- honesty
- emotional safety

Hard conversations become easier when you stop trying to win and start trying to understand.

᧙ What People Are Really Saying in Hard Conversations

Most people don't speak in needs — they speak in reactions.

Behind:

"You hurt me." is often **"I needed something different."**

Behind:

"You don't care." is often **"I feel disconnected."**

Behind:

"I'm done." is often **"I'm overwhelmed and don't know how to stay."**

Behind:

"Why would you say that?" is often **"I feel unsafe."**

Behind:

Silence is often **"I don't know how to express this without losing you."**

Hard conversations require listening beneath the words.

᧙ How to Prepare for a Hard Conversation

Preparation is not scripting — it's grounding.

Before you speak:

1. Regulate your body

Slow your breath. Relax your shoulders. Unclench your jaw.

2. Identify your intention

"What do I want to create — clarity, connection, repair, understanding?"

3. Notice your intention style

"Which part of me is rising — Protector, Pleaser, Performer, Prover, Peace-maker, Planner, or Processor?"

4. Choose your truth

"What is the clearest, kindest version of what I need to say?"
    Grounding prepares your nervous system for honesty.

℘ How to Begin a Hard Conversation

The beginning sets the tone.
    Start with:

- intention
- clarity
- compassion
- emotional safety

It sounds like:

- "I want to talk about something important because I care about us."
- "This conversation matters to me, and I want to approach it gently."
- "I'm not trying to blame — I'm trying to understand."
- "Can we talk about something that's been on my heart?"

These openings soften defenses and create space for truth.

∽ How Each Intention Style Navigates Hard Conversations

Protector: Practice softening your tone before speaking.

Pleaser: Practice naming your needs without apologizing.

Performer: Practice speaking honestly instead of perfectly.

Prover: Practice listening without defending.

Peacemaker: Practice staying present instead of disappearing.

Planner: Practice letting the conversation unfold naturally.

Processor: Practice saying, "I need a moment to think," instead of shutting down.

Your intention style becomes a strength when led with awareness.

∽ Scripts for Hard Conversations

When you need to express hurt

"I care about us, and something you said felt painful. Can we talk about it?"

When you need clarity

"I'm confused about what happened. Can you help me understand?"

When you feel overwhelmed

"I want to stay in this conversation, and I need a moment to breathe."

When you need to set a boundary

"I want to keep talking, but not in this tone."

When you need to repair

"I reacted from my trigger, not my truth. I'd like to try again."

When you need honesty

"I've been holding something in, and I want to share it gently."
Scripts don't replace authenticity — they support it.

᠀ Tools for Navigating Emotional Intensity

1. The Centered Pause

A breath before responding.

2. The "I + I" Formula

Impact + Intention "I see the impact of what I said, and here was my intention."

3. The Slow-Down Signal

"Can we slow this down so we can hear each other?"

4. The Reset Phrase

"Let's pause and try again."

5. The Return Plan

"I need a moment. I will come back."
These tools keep the conversation grounded.

✐ How to Stay Connected During Conflict

Connection is not agreement — it is presence.
You stay connected by:

- softening your tone
- validating feelings
- asking clarifying questions
- naming your intention
- staying curious
- avoiding assumptions
- returning to repair

Connection is a choice, not a coincidence.

✐ Closing Thought

Hard conversations are not the enemy — avoidance is. Hard conversations are not the threat — silence is. Hard conversations are not the problem — disconnection is.
When you navigate conflict, disappointment, and emotional intensity with intention:

- clarity rises
- compassion deepens
- repair becomes possible
- trust grows
- connection strengthens

Hard conversations become healing conversations when you lead with presence, truth, and emotional safety.

This is how you communicate with intention — even when it's hard.

🌿 Reflection Prompts

✧ Self-Reflection

- What makes hard conversations difficult for me?
- Which intention style takes over when emotions rise?
- What helps me stay grounded during conflict?
- What truth have I been avoiding that needs gentle expression?

✧ Connection Reflection

- How do others respond when I approach hard conversations with clarity and compassion?
- What phrase or tool helps me stay connected during emotional intensity?
- What hard conversation this week could benefit from more intention and presence?

CHAPTER 20 SUMMARY — IN HARD CONVERSATIONS

- Hard conversations reveal what matters.
- Your intention style shapes how you respond under pressure.
- Preparation, grounding, and clarity make conflict safer.
- Scripts and tools help you navigate emotional intensity.
- Hard conversations become healing conversations when led with intention.

V

🌿 Part V — Legacy

Every word we speak leaves something behind.
Long after the conversation ends, long after the moment passes,
long after the people in the room have moved on, our words
continue to shape how others feel, how they see themselves, and
how they remember us. Communication is not just a skill — it is a
form of legacy.
In this final section, we step into the deeper truth of intentional
communication: your words are seeds.
They take root in the people you love. They grow in the spaces
you lead.

21

The Language You Leave Behind

How your words shape identity, memory, and generational healing

Legacy is not built in grand gestures — it is built in the quiet, consistent language you speak every day.

Your words become the stories your children tell about themselves. Your tone becomes the way they talk to their own hearts. Your presence becomes the emotional blueprint they carry into adulthood. Your communication becomes the inheritance they pass to the next generation.

This chapter is about the language you leave behind — the words that shape identity, the tone that shapes memory, and the intentional communication that becomes generational healing.

Legacy Lives in Language

Legacy is not just what you *do* — it's what you *say*.

Your words become:

- the voice your children hear in their quiet moments
- the reassurance they reach for when life feels heavy
- the boundaries they learn to set
- the compassion they learn to offer
- the truth they learn to speak

- the safety they learn to expect

Language is the first inheritance. And the most lasting.

↷ The Emotional Echo of Your Words

Every word you speak carries an emotional echo.

Some words echo safety. Some words echo fear. Some words echo shame. Some words echo belonging. Some words echo possibility.

Children don't forget how your words made them feel — they carry that feeling into every relationship they build.

Your language becomes their internal narrator.

↷ How Intention Styles Shape the Legacy You Leave

Your intention styles influence the emotional tone of your legacy:

The Protector leaves a legacy of strength — but sometimes sharpness. **The Pleaser** leaves a legacy of kindness — but sometimes self-erasure. **The Performer** leaves a legacy of excellence — but sometimes pressure. **The Prover** leaves a legacy of clarity — but sometimes rigidity. **The Peacemaker** leaves a legacy of calm — but sometimes silence. **The Planner** leaves a legacy of structure — but sometimes control. **The Processor** leaves a legacy of thoughtfulness — but sometimes distance.

When led with intention, each style becomes a gift. When led by fear, each style becomes a wound.

Legacy is shaped by which part of you speaks the loudest.

↷ The Language That Heals Generations

Healing language is intentional language. It sounds like:

- "I see you."
- "Your feelings matter."

- "You don't have to be perfect."
- "You are safe with me."
- "I'm proud of you."
- "Let's try again together."
- "You can tell me the truth."
- "I love who you are becoming."

These words don't just comfort the moment — they rewrite the story.

They become the emotional foundation your children stand on. They become the voice they use with their own children. They become the healing that outlives you.

✒ The Language That Hurts — And How to Transform It

Unintentional language often comes from:

- exhaustion
- overwhelm
- fear
- old wounds
- inherited patterns

It sounds like:

- "Stop crying."
- "You're too sensitive."
- "You should know better."
- "Why can't you just…?"
- "I don't have time for this."

These words don't make you a bad parent or partner — they make you a human one.

Legacy is not about never getting it wrong. Legacy is about repairing when you do.

Transforming harmful language begins with:

- awareness
- apology
- intention
- new patterns
- gentler words

Healing begins the moment you choose a different sentence.

℘ Your Words Become Their Inner Voice

The way you speak to the people you love becomes the way they speak to themselves.

When you say:

"You're capable," they learn confidence.

When you say:

"It's okay to feel," they learn emotional safety.

When you say:

"You don't have to rush," they learn patience.

When you say:

"I'm here," they learn belonging.

Your voice becomes their compass.

℘ practices for Leaving a Healing Legacy

1. The Daily Affirmation Ritual

One sentence spoken consistently: "You are loved, and you are enough."

2. The Repair Ritual

After conflict: "I'm sorry for my tone. You matter to me."

3. The Naming Ritual

Help them name their feelings: "You're feeling frustrated — that makes sense."

4. The Blessing Ritual

Before bed or before school: "May you feel brave, kind, and grounded today."

5. The Story Ritual

Share family stories that honor resilience, not shame.
  practices turn language into memory. Memory turns language into legacy.

෴ How to Speak Legacy Into the Next Generation

Legacy language is:

- slow
- intentional
- compassionate
- clear
- grounded
- emotionally safe

It sounds like:
  "I want you to know who you are." "I want you to feel safe in your own voice." "I want you to trust your feelings." "I want you to grow without fear." "I want you to inherit healing, not hurt."

Legacy is not what you leave *to* them — it's what you leave *in* them.

◌ Closing Thought

Your words are seeds. Some grow immediately. Some grow years later. Some grow in your children. Some grow in their children. Some grow in the people who were never in the room but were shaped by the people who were shaped by you.

This is the power of intentional communication. This is the power of emotional safety. This is the power of legacy.

The language you speak today becomes the healing they carry tomorrow.

❧ Reflection Prompts

✦ Self-Reflection

- What language did I inherit that I want to transform?
- Which intention style shapes my communication legacy most strongly?
- What words do I want my children or community to remember?
- What tone do I want to be known for?

✦ Connection Reflection

- How do others respond when I speak with intention and emotional safety?
- What phrase or ritual could strengthen the legacy I'm building?
- What relationship in my life needs more healing language this week?

CHAPTER 21 SUMMARY — THE LANGUAGE YOU LEAVE BEHIND

- Your words become identity, memory, and inheritance.
- Each intention style shapes the emotional tone of your legacy.

- Healing language rewrites generational patterns.
- Your voice becomes their inner voice.
- Legacy is not what you leave *to* them — but what you leave *in* them.

149

22

Daily Practices for Intentional Communicators

Practices, reflections, and affirmations

Intentional communication is not a skill you master once — it is a practice you return to daily.

It is the way you breathe before you speak. The way you pause before reacting. The way you choose clarity over confusion. The way you repair instead of retreat. The way you speak to yourself before you speak to others.

This chapter offers daily practices, reflections, and affirmations that help you stay grounded in your intention, connected to your truth, and aligned with the legacy you want to leave behind.

These practices are simple, repeatable, and powerful — because transformation happens in the small moments you choose differently.

⸿ Why Daily Practice Matters

Your intention styles don't disappear — they soften through repetition.

Your nervous system doesn't regulate once — it regulates through rhythm.

Your communication doesn't transform in a single conversation — it transforms through consistent, intentional choices.

Daily practice helps you:

- stay grounded
- stay aware
- stay connected
- stay compassionate
- stay aligned with your values
- stay anchored in your truth

Practice is how intention becomes instinct.

௸ Daily practices for Intentional Communicators

These practices are designed to be short, accessible, and deeply grounding.

1. The Morning Centering Practice

Before you speak to anyone else, speak to yourself.

Place a hand on your heart and say:

"Today, I choose clarity. Today, I choose compassion. Today, I choose intention."

This sets the emotional tone for your day.

2. The Breath-Before-Response Practice

One slow breath before you speak.

Inhale: *I'm safe.* Exhale: *I can respond with intention.*

This single breath can change the entire conversation.

3. The Tone Check Practice

Ask yourself:

"What tone am I bringing into this moment?"

Tone is the emotional doorway. This ritual keeps you aware of what you're carrying.

4. The "Name It" Practice

Name your emotion before it names your reaction.
"I'm feeling overwhelmed." "I'm feeling anxious." "I'm feeling hopeful."
Naming creates clarity. Clarity creates safety.

5. The Daily Repair Practice

Every evening, ask:
"Is there anything I need to repair before I rest?"
Repair keeps resentment from growing roots.

6. The Gratitude Language Practice

Speak one sentence of appreciation to someone each day.
"I'm grateful for you." "I noticed your effort." "I appreciate your presence."
Gratitude strengthens connection.

7. The Boundary Check Practice

Ask yourself:
"What boundary do I need to honor today?"
This keeps you aligned with your emotional well-being.

๑ Daily Reflections for Intentional Communicators

Reflection turns experience into wisdom.
Here are simple prompts you can use each morning or evening:

- What intention style led me today?
- When did I speak from my truth?
- When did I speak from my trigger?

- What moment am I proud of?
- What moment needs repair?
- What did my body feel like during hard conversations?
- What do I want to practice tomorrow?

Reflection is how you learn your patterns with compassion, not judgment.

Daily Affirmations for Each Intention Style

Affirmations help you lead your style instead of being led by it.

Protector

"I can be strong and soft at the same time."

Pleaser

"My needs matter just as much as theirs."

Performer

"I don't have to be perfect to be worthy."

Prover

"I can release the need to defend."

Peacemaker

"My voice deserves space too."

Planner

"I can trust the moment even when it's uncertain."

Processor

"I can take my time and stay connected."

Affirmations help your nervous system trust new patterns.

ᢙ Affirmations for Daily Communication

These can be spoken aloud, written in a journal, or repeated silently:

- "I communicate with clarity and compassion."
- "I choose presence over reaction."
- "I honor my truth and respect yours."
- "I can pause without disconnecting."
- "I repair quickly and gently."
- "I speak from intention, not fear."
- "My words create safety."
- "My communication is part of my legacy."

Affirmations shape your inner voice — your inner voice shapes your outer communication.

ᢙ A Simple Daily Practice: The Intention Check-In

At any moment, ask yourself:

"What am I trying to create right now?"

Connection? Clarity? Understanding? Repair? Honesty? Safety?

This single question brings you back to your center.

๙ Closing Thought

Intentional communication is not about perfection — it is about practice.

Every breath, every pause, every repair, every boundary, every gentle word becomes part of your emotional legacy.

Your daily practices shape:

- your relationships
- your home
- your leadership
- your community
- your children
- your future
- your healing

The language you practice today becomes the legacy you leave tomorrow.

๙ Reflection Prompts

✧ Self-Reflection

- Which daily ritual supports me the most right now?
- What intention style needs the most attention this week?
- What affirmation feels most grounding to me?
- What practice helps me return to my center?

✧ Connection Reflection

- How do others respond when I practice intentional communication daily?
- What ritual could strengthen my relationships this week?
- What moment today could benefit from a breath, a pause, or a reset?

CHAPTER 22 SUMMARY — DAILY PRACTICES FOR INTENTIONAL COMMU-NICATORS

- Daily practices turn intention into instinct.
- Reflection transforms patterns into wisdom.
- Affirmations shape your inner voice and your legacy.
- Small, consistent practices create emotional safety.
- Your daily choices become your generational impact.

VI

Apendices

Appendix A — Conversation Scripts

Gentle, grounded language for real-life moments

These scripts are not meant to be repeated word-for-word. They are scaffolding — a starting point for your own voice.

ꞕ 1. When You Need a Pause

"I want to respond with care, not reaction. Can we pause for a moment so I can gather my thoughts?"

"I'm feeling overwhelmed. I need a few minutes to breathe before we continue."

ꞕ 2. When You Need Clarity

"I want to make sure I understand. Can you tell me what you meant by that?"

"I'm hearing a few things at once. What's the most important part for you?"

ꞕ 3. When You Need a Boundary

"I'm not available for that today, but I can revisit it later."
   "I care about this conversation, and I need us to speak respectfully."

᧽ 4. When You Need to Express a Feeling

"I'm feeling anxious, and I want to talk about this calmly."
"I'm hurt, and I want us to understand each other better."

᧽ 5. When You Need to Repair

"I'm sorry for my tone earlier. I want to try again with more care."
"I see how my words impacted you. Thank you for telling me."

᧽ 6. When Someone Else Is Upset

"I hear you. Your feelings make sense."
"I want to understand what this felt like for you."

᧽ 7. When You Need to Say No

"Thank you for thinking of me. I don't have the capacity right now."
"I can't commit to that, but I hope it goes well."

᧽ 8. When You Need to Ask for Support

"I'm carrying a lot today. Could you help me with...?"
"I need clarity and reassurance right now."

᧽ 9. When You Need to Address Tension

"Something felt off earlier. Can we talk about it so we can move forward?"
"I value our relationship, and I want to clear this up."

✤ 10. When You Need to Affirm Someone

"I'm proud of you."
 "You handled that with so much grace."
 "I see your effort, and it matters."

Appendix B — Intention Style Self-Assessment

A gentle tool for understanding your communication patterns
This assessment helps identify your primary intention style — not to label them, but to illuminate patterns and open pathways for growth.

For each statement, rate how true it feels on a scale of 1–5:
1 = Not at all true 5 = Very true

ᛜ The Protector

______ I become defensive when I feel misunderstood.
______ I raise my voice or sharpen my tone when I feel threatened.
______ I try to stay in control of the conversation.
______ I struggle to show vulnerability in conflict.
______ I react quickly when I feel emotionally unsafe.
Protector Score: ______

ᛜ The Pleaser

______ I avoid saying no even when I'm overwhelmed.
______ I soften my needs to keep others comfortable.
______ I feel anxious when someone is disappointed in me.
______ I often apologize even when I've done nothing wrong.
______ I prioritize harmony over honesty.
Pleaser Score: ______

♔ The Performer

_______ I try to stay upbeat even when I'm struggling.

_______ I hide my true feelings to avoid burdening others.

_______ I feel pressure to "hold it together" for everyone.

_______ I worry about being seen as too emotional.

_______ I shift into "presentation mode" when conversations get tense.

Performer Score: _______

♔ The Prover

_______ I explain myself in great detail to avoid being misunderstood.

_______ I feel the need to justify my decisions.

_______ I get stuck in the facts instead of the feelings.

_______ I talk more when I feel anxious.

_______ I feel uncomfortable when conversations lack clarity or logic.

Prover Score: _______

♔ The Peacemaker

_______ I shut down or withdraw when conflict arises.

_______ I avoid hard conversations to keep the peace.

_______ I struggle to express my needs directly.

_______ I feel overwhelmed by emotional intensity.

_______ I stay quiet to prevent tension, even when something matters to me.

Peacemaker Score: _______

♔ The Planner

_______ I try to organize or fix the conversation.

_______ I feel anxious when things feel unpredictable.

_______ I take responsibility for everyone's emotional state.

_______ I struggle to let go of control.

_______ I mentally rehearse conversations before they happen.
Planner Score: _______

๛ The Processor

_______ I turn inward and need time before responding.
_______ I replay conversations in my mind to understand what happened.
_______ I freeze or go quiet when emotions rise quickly.
_______ I communicate more clearly after I've had space to think.
_______ I feel pressured when asked to respond immediately.
Processor Score: _______

๛ Interpreting Your Results

Your highest score is your **primary intention style**. Your second-highest score is your **secondary style** — the one that shows up under stress.

This assessment is not about judgment.

It's about awareness — the first step toward intentional communication.

After completing the assessment, total the score for each intention style.

Each style will fall into one of these ranges:

5–10: Dormant Pattern

This style is present in you, but it doesn't lead your communication. It may show up occasionally, usually in mild stress or specific environments.

11–15: Active Pattern

This style influences your communication regularly. You'll notice it in everyday interactions and especially when you're tired, overwhelmed, or emotionally stretched.

16–20: Dominant Pattern

This style is your primary communication instinct. It shapes your tone, reactions, boundaries, and emotional habits. It's not "good" or "bad" — it's simply your starting point.

21–25: Intensified Pattern

This style is deeply ingrained and likely developed from early experiences, family patterns, or long-term coping strategies. It may feel automatic or hard to interrupt — but it is absolutely workable with awareness and intention.

๛ THE PROTECTOR

When safety becomes silence or defensiveness

5–10: Dormant Protector

You rarely become defensive and generally feel safe expressing yourself.

11–15: Active Protector

You protect yourself when conversations feel tense or unclear.

16–20: Dominant Protector

You often guard your emotions and may react quickly when you feel misunderstood.

21–25: Intensified Protector

You learned early to defend yourself. Your instinct is to shield, withdraw, or control the tone of the room.

๛ THE PLEASER

How over-accommodation erodes authenticity

5–10: Dormant Pleaser

You can say no comfortably and rarely overextend.

11–15: Active Pleaser

You want harmony and sometimes soften your needs to maintain it.

16–20: Dominant Pleaser

You often prioritize others' comfort over your own truth.

21–25: Intensified Pleaser

You learned to earn safety through compliance. Disappointing others feels emotionally risky.

℘ THE PERFORMER

When communication becomes a stage instead of a bridge

5–10: Dormant Performer

You feel comfortable being authentic without managing others' perceptions.

11–15: Active Performer

You bring positivity but sometimes hide your true feelings.

16–20: Dominant Performer

You often mask your emotions to avoid burdening others.

21–25: Intensified Performer

You learned to survive by being "on." Vulnerability feels unsafe or unfamiliar.

℘ THE PROVER

The need to be right and how it blocks connection

5–10: Dormant Prover

You rarely feel the need to explain or justify yourself.

11–15: Active Prover

You value clarity and sometimes over-explain to avoid misunderstanding.

16–20: Dominant Prover

You often rely on logic, details, or facts to feel secure in communication.

21–25: Intensified Prover

You learned that being right meant being safe. Emotional conversations feel uncertain or uncomfortable.

ɡ THE PEACEMAKER

Avoiding conflict at the cost of clarity

5–10: Dormant Peacemaker

You can handle conflict without shutting down.

11–15: Active Peacemaker

You prefer calm and may avoid tension when you're tired.

16–20: Dominant Peacemaker

You often withdraw, shut down, or stay quiet to keep the peace.

21–25: Intensified Peacemaker

You learned that conflict was unsafe. Silence became your shield.

ɡ THE PLANNER

Controlling outcomes instead of engaging in presence

5–10: Dormant Planner

You can flow with conversations without needing control.

11–15: Active Planner

You like structure and clarity and sometimes take charge to reduce uncertainty.

16–20: Dominant Planner

You often manage the emotional or logistical direction of conversations.

21–25: Intensified Planner

You learned to stay safe by anticipating everything. Unpredictability feels threatening.

ɡ THE PROCESSOR

Turning inward before responding

5–10: Dormant Processor

You communicate easily in the moment and rarely freeze.

11–15: Active Processor

You need a little time to think before responding clearly.

16–20: Dominant Processor

You often go inward, replay conversations, or need space to articulate your thoughts.

21–25: Intensified Processor

You learned to internalize emotions. Speaking in the moment feels overwhelming or unsafe.

Appendix C — Reflection Prompts

Questions to deepen self-awareness and strengthen communication

These prompts can be used daily, weekly, or whenever readers need ground-ing.

⚘ Self-Awareness

- What emotion do I avoid expressing most often?
- What situations pull me out of my center?
- What helps me return to calm?

⚘ Relationships

- What conversations am I avoiding, and why?
- What boundary would bring me more peace?
- What repair is asking for my attention?

⚘ Intention Styles

- Which intention style shows up when I'm overwhelmed?
- What does my body feel like when I'm triggered?
- What intention do I want to lead with more often?

❧ Legacy

- What emotional patterns am I rewriting?
- What do I want my words to leave behind?
- How do I want people to feel after talking to me?

Appendix D — About the Author

Donise is a life coach, communicator, and legacy-builder who helps families, communities, and leaders create emotionally safe environments through intentional communication. She blends neuroscience, storytelling, and lived experience to teach others how to respond with clarity, compassion, and grounded presence.

As the creator of *The Unprofessional Mom*, Donise equips mothers with tools to break generational patterns, nurture emotional safety, and raise children who feel seen and supported. Her work is known for its warmth, honesty, and practical wisdom — a reflection of the women who shaped her and the legacy she is committed to carrying forward.

Donise lives her message daily as a wife, mother, life coach, and community leader. Her passion is simple and profound: **to help people speak in ways that build, not break — and to leave a legacy of healing through language.**